TIMOTHY D. KANOLD
Series Editor

BEYOND THE COMMON CORE

A HANDBOOK FOR

Mathematics

in a PLC at Work™

GRADES K–5

Solution Tree | Press

A Joint Publication With

 NCTM | NATIONAL COUNCIL OF TEACHERS OF MATHEMATICS

Juli K. Dixon
Thomasenia Lott Adams
Edward C. Nolan

D0473180

555 North Morton Street
Bloomington, IN 47404
800.733.6786 (toll free) / 812.336.7700
FAX: 812.336.7790

email: info@solution-tree.com
solution-tree.com

Visit **go.solution-tree.com/mathematicsatwork** to download the reproducibles in this book.

Printed in the United States of America

18 17 16 15 14   1 2 3 4 5

Library of Congress Cataloging-in-Publication Data

Dixon, Juli K., author.
  Beyond the common core : a handbook for mathematics in a PLC at work, grades K-5 / Juli K. Dixon, Thomasenia Lott Adams, Edward C. Nolan ; Timothy D. Kanold (editor).
      pages cm. -- (Beyond the common core)
  Includes bibliographical references and index.
  ISBN 978-1-936763-46-7 (perfect bound) 1. Mathematics--Study and teaching (Primary)--Standards--United States.
2. Mathematics--Study and teaching (Elementary)--Standards--United States. 3. Professional learning communities.
I. Adams, Thomasenia Lott, author. II. Nolan, Edward C., author. III. Kanold, Timothy D., editor. IV. Title.
  QA135.6.D59 2015
  372.7--dc23
                            2014024875

Solution Tree
Jeffrey C. Jones, CEO
Edmund M. Ackerman, President

Solution Tree Press
President: Douglas M. Rife
Associate Acquisitions Editor: Kari Gillesse
Editorial Director: Lesley Bolton
Managing Production Editor: Caroline Weiss
Senior Production Editor: Suzanne Kraszcwski
Copy Editor: Sarah Payne-Mills
Proofreader: Elisabeth Abrams
Text and Cover Designer: Laura Kagemann
Compositor: Rachel Smith

Acknowledgments

My deepest love and gratitude to my daughters, Alex and Jessica, who continue to allow me to understand mathematics more deeply through their eyes, and to my husband, Marc, who understands my need to spend countless hours doing so. Special thanks to all of the teachers who have used our books and helped us to see how to extend their learning. And finally, to our mentor, Tim Kanold, thank you for providing the opportunity to help so many.

—Juli K. Dixon

My accomplishments would not be possible without the support I receive from my husband of twenty-five years, Larry, and from our three sons, Blake, Philip, and Kurt, or without the love of my father, Pickens Lott, Jr. (deceased), and my mother, Tennie Ruth Lott, and the daily strength that comes by way of knowing who I belong to.

—Thomasenia Lott Adams

Many thanks to my family, Michele and Calvin, for the wonderful support they provide me in all of my endeavors. I also wish to thank all of my colleagues from whom I have learned so much over the years.

—Edward C. Nolan

First and foremost, I extend thanks to Juli, Thomasenia, and Ed for understanding the joy, the pain, and the hard work of the writing journey, and for giving freely of their talent to others. Thanks, too, to Jeff Jones and Douglas Rife from Solution Tree for their belief in our vision and work in mathematics education. Special thanks to Becky DuFour for her wisdom, insight, advice, and deep understanding of what it takes to become an authentic professional learning community. Most importantly, thanks to Susan, my loving critic, who understands how to formatively guide me through a handbook series as bold as this.

—Timothy D. Kanold

Solution Tree Press would like to thank the following reviewers:

Kristopher J. Childs
Project Director, The Cognitively Guided Instruction Project
University of Central Florida
Orlando, Florida

Matt Larson
Mathematics Curriculum Specialist
Lincoln Public Schools
Lincoln, Nebraska

Samantha Neff
Mathematics Coach
Highlands Elementary
Winter Springs, Florida

George J. Roy
Assistant Professor, Middle Level Mathematics Education
University of South Carolina
Columbia, South Carolina

Farshid Safi
Associate Professor, Mathematics Education
The College of New Jersey
Ewing Township, New Jersey

Sarah Schuhl
PLC Associate and Mathematics Educational Consultant
Portland, Oregon

Jennifer M. Tobias
Assistant Professor, Department of Mathematics
Illinois State University
Normal, Illinois

James Vreeland
Director of Mathematics and Science
School District 54
Schaumburg, Illinois

Visit **go.solution-tree.com/mathematicsatwork** to download the reproducibles in this book.

Table of Contents

About the Editor

Timothy D. Kanold, PhD, is an award-winning educator, author, and consultant. He is former director of mathematics and science and served as superintendent of Adlai E. Stevenson High School District 125, a model professional learning community district in Lincolnshire, Illinois. He serves as an adjunct faculty member for the graduate school at Loyola University Chicago.

Dr. Kanold is committed to a vision for Mathematics at Work™, a process of learning and working together that builds knowledge sharing, equity, and excellence for all students, faculty, and school administrators. He conducts highly motivational professional development leadership seminars worldwide with a focus on turning school vision into realized action that creates increased learning opportunities for students through the effective delivery of professional learning communities for faculty and administrators.

He is a past president of the National Council of Supervisors of Mathematics and coauthor of several best-selling mathematics textbooks. He has served on writing commissions for the National Council of Teachers of Mathematics and the National Council of Supervisors of Mathematics. He has authored numerous articles and chapters on school mathematics, leadership, and professional development for education publications.

In 2010, Dr. Kanold received the prestigious international Damen Award for outstanding contributions to the leadership field of education from Loyola University Chicago. He also received the Outstanding Administrator Award from the Illinois State Board of Education in 1994 and the Presidential Award for Excellence in Mathematics and Science Teaching in 1986.

Dr. Kanold earned a bachelor's degree in education and a master's degree in applied mathematics from Illinois State University. He completed a master's in educational administration at the University of Illinois and received a doctorate in educational leadership and counseling psychology from Loyola University Chicago.

To learn more about Dr. Kanold's work, visit his blog *Turning Vision Into Action* at http://tkanold .blogspot.com, or follow @tkanold on Twitter.

To book Dr. Kanold for professional development, contact pd@solution-tree.com.

About the Authors

Juli K. Dixon, PhD, is a professor of mathematics education at the University of Central Florida (UCF) in Orlando. She coordinates the award-winning Lockheed Martin/UCF Academy for Mathematics and Science for the K–8 master of education program as well as the mathematics track of the doctoral program in education. Prior to joining the faculty at UCF, Dr. Dixon was a secondary mathematics educator at the University of Nevada–Las Vegas and a public school mathematics teacher in urban school settings at the elementary, middle, and secondary levels.

She is a prolific writer who has authored and coauthored books, textbooks, chapters, and articles. She is a coauthor of school mathematics textbooks for grades ranging from kindergarten to high school. A sought-after speaker, Dr. Dixon has delivered keynotes and other presentations throughout the United States. She has served as chair of the National Council of Teachers of Mathematics Student Explorations in Mathematics Editorial Panel and as a board member for the Association of Mathematics Teacher Educators. At the state level, she has served on the board of directors for the Nevada Mathematics Council and is past president of the Florida Association of Mathematics Teacher Educators.

Dr. Dixon earned a bachelor's degree in mathematics and education from SUNY–Potsdam, a master's degree in mathematics education from Syracuse University, and a doctorate in curriculum and instruction with an emphasis in mathematics education from the University of Florida.

Thomasenia Lott Adams, PhD, is an associate dean and professor of mathematics education in the College of Education at the University of Florida. She has mentored many future teachers of mathematics and mathematics teacher educators. She is the author of an elementary mathematics text series, academic books, and numerous refereed journal articles. Dr. Adams is a nationally known presenter at conferences and for professional development in school settings, which often includes teaching mathematics in grades K–8. She is a trained National School Reform Faculty Certified Critical Friends Group Coach.

Dr. Adams previously served as editor for the Mathematical Roots Department in *Mathematics Teaching in the Middle School* and coeditor for the Investigations Department of *Teaching Children Mathematics*. She is a past board member for the Association of Mathematics Teacher Educators and School Science and Mathematics Association. She is also a past president of the Florida Association of Mathematics Teacher Educators and recipient of the Mary L. Collins Teacher Educator of the Year Award from the Florida Association of Teacher Educators.

She has engaged in many high-impact mathematics education projects, including Algebra Nation, an online platform for supporting the teaching and learning of algebra. Dr. Adams was the team leader for mathematics and science job-embedded professional development for middle and high school mathematics and science teachers.

She earned a bachelor of science in mathematics from South Carolina State University and a master of education and doctorate of philosophy in instruction and curriculum with an emphasis in mathematics education from the University of Florida.

 **Edward C. Nolan** is preK–12 director of mathematics for Montgomery County Public Schools in Maryland. He has nineteen years of classroom experience in both middle and high schools and was department chair for fifteen years. An active member of the National Council of Teachers of Mathematics, he is president-elect of the Maryland Council of Supervisors of Mathematics. Nolan is also a consultant for Solution Tree and the Resident Teacher Professional Preparation Program at the University of Central Florida, where he provides support for preservice teachers and their in-service mentors on the Common Core State Standards for mathematics.

Nolan has been published in the *Banneker Banner*, a publication of the Maryland Council of Teachers of Mathematics, and *Mathematics Teaching in the Middle School*, a publication of the National Council of Teachers of Mathematics (NCTM), and he has conducted professional development at the state, regional, and national levels, including webinars for NCTM and TODOS: Mathematics for ALL. His research interests lie in supporting students in developing algebraic thinking and reasoning. In 2005, Nolan won the Presidential Award for Excellence in Mathematics and Science Teaching.

He is a graduate of the University of Maryland. He earned a master's degree in educational administration from Western Maryland College.

To book Juli K. Dixon, Thomasenia Lott Adams, or Edward C. Nolan for professional development, contact pd@solution-tree.com.

Introduction

You have high impact on the front lines as you snag children in the river of life.

—Tracy Kidder

Your work as an elementary school mathematics teacher is one of the most important, and at the same time, one of the most difficult jobs to do well in education. Since the release of our 2012 Solution Tree Press series *Common Core Mathematics in a PLC at Work™*, our authors, reviewers, school leaders, and consultants from the Mathematics at Work™ team have had the opportunity to work with thousands of grades K–5 teachers and teacher teams from across the United States who are just like you: educators trying to urgently and consistently seek deeper and more meaningful solutions to a sustained effort for meeting the challenge of improved student learning. From California to Virginia, Utah to Florida, Oregon to New York, Wisconsin to Texas, and beyond, we have discovered a thirst for implementation of K–12 mathematics programs that will sustain student success over time. A focus on the elementary grades is a significant component of the K–12 effort toward improved student learning.

Certainly, the Common Core State Standards (CCSS) for mathematics have served as a catalyst for much of the national focus and conversation about improving student learning. However, your essential work as a teacher of grades K–5 mathematics and as part of a collaborative team in your local school and district takes you *beyond* your state's standards—whatever they may be. As the authors of the National Council of Teachers of Mathematics (Leinwand et al., 2014) publication *Principles to Actions: Ensuring Mathematical Success for All* argue, standards in and of themselves do not describe the essential conditions necessary to ensure mathematics learning for all students. You, as the classroom teacher, are the most important ingredient to student success.

Thus, this K–5 mathematics teaching and assessing handbook is designed to take you *beyond the product* of standards themselves by providing you and your collaborative team with the guidance, support, and *process* tools necessary to achieve mathematics program greatness within the context of higher levels of demonstrated student learning and performance.

Whether you are from a state that is participating in one of the CCSS assessment consortia or from a state that uses a unique mathematics assessment designed only for that state, it is our hope that this handbook provides a continual process that allows you to move toward a local program of great mathematics teaching and learning for you and your students.

Your daily work in mathematics begins by understanding that what does make a significant difference (in terms of high levels of student achievement) are the thousands of instructional and assessment decisions you and your collaborative team will make every year—every day and in every unit.

The Grain Size of Change Is the Teacher Team

We believe that the best strategy to achieve the expectations of CCSS-type state standards is to create schools and districts that operate as professional learning communities (PLCs), and, more specifically, within a PLC at Work™ culture as outlined by Richard DuFour, Robert Eaker, Rebecca DuFour, and

Tom Many (2010). We believe that the PLC process supports a grain size of change that is just right—not too small (the individual teacher) and not too big (the district office)—for impacting deep change. The adult knowledge capacity development and growth necessary to deliver on the promise of standards that expect student demonstrations of understanding reside in the engine that drives the PLC school culture: the teacher team.

There is a never-ending aspect to your professional journey and the high-leverage teacher and teacher team actions that measure your impact on student learning. This idea is at the very heart of your work. As John Hattie (2012) states in *Visible Learning for Teachers: Maximizing Impact on Learning*:

> My role as a teacher is to evaluate the effect I have on my students. It is to "know thy impact," it is to understand this impact, and it is to act on this knowing and understanding. This requires that teachers gather defensible and dependable evidence from many sources, and hold collaborative discussions with colleagues and students about this evidence, thus making the effect of their teaching visible to themselves and to others. (p. 19)

Knowing Your Vision for Mathematics Instruction and Assessment

Quick—you have thirty seconds: turn to a colleague and declare your vision for mathematics instruction and assessment in your school. What exactly will you say? More importantly, on a scale of 1 (low) to 6 (high), what would be the degree of coherence between your and your colleagues' visions for instruction and assessment?

We have asked these vision questions to more than one thousand mathematics teachers across the United States since 2011, and the answers have been consistent: wide variance on assessment coherence (low scores of 1, 2, or 3 mostly) and general agreement that the idea of some type of a formative assessment process is supposed to be in your vision for mathematics instruction and assessment.

A favorite team exercise we use to capture the vision for instruction and assessment is to ask a team of three to five teachers to draw a circle in the middle of a sheet of poster paper. We ask each team member to write a list (outside of the circle) of three or four vital adult behaviors that reflect his or her vision for instruction and assessment. After brainstorming, the team will have twelve to fifteen vital teacher behaviors.

We then ask the team to prepare its vision for mathematics instruction and assessment inside the circle. The vision must represent the vital behaviors each team member has listed in eighteen words or less. We indicate, too, that the vision should describe a "compelling picture of the school's future that produces energy, passion, and action in yourself and others" (Kanold, 2011, p. 12).

Team members are allowed to use pictures, phrases, or complete sentences, but all together, the vision cannot be more than eighteen words. Often, in our workshops, professional development events, conferences, institutes, and onsite work, we have been asked a simple, yet complex question: *"How?"* How do you begin to make decisions and do your work in ways that will advance your vision for mathematics instruction and assessment in your elementary school? How do you honor what is inside your circle? And how do you know that your circle, your defined vision for mathematics instruction and assessment, represents the "right things" to pursue that are worthy of your best energy and effort?

In our *Common Core Mathematics in a PLC at Work* (2012) grades K–2 and grades 3–5 books, we explain how understanding *formative assessment* as a research-affirmed *process* for student and adult learning serves as a catalyst for successful CCSS mathematics content implementation. In the series, we establish the pursuit of assessment as a process of formative feedback and learning for the students and the adults as a highly effective practice to pursue (see chapter 4 in Kanold, Larson, Fennell, Adams, Dixon, Kobett, & Wray, 2012a, 2012b).

In this handbook, our Mathematics at Work team provides tools for *how* to achieve that collaborative pursuit: how to engage in ten *high-leverage team actions* (HLTAs) steeped in a commitment to a vision for mathematics instruction and assessment that will result in greater student learning than ever before.

A Cycle for Analysis and Learning: The Instructional Unit

The mathematics unit or chapter of content creates a natural cycle of manageable time for a teacher's and team's work throughout the year. What is a *unit*? For the purposes of your work in this handbook, we define a *unit* as a chunk of mathematics content. It might be a chapter from your textbook or other materials for the course, a part of a chapter or set of materials, or a combination of various short chapters or content materials. A unit generally lasts no less than two to three weeks and no more than four to five weeks.

As DuFour, Eaker, and DuFour (2008), the architects of the PLC at Work process, advise, there are four critical questions every collaborative team in a PLC at Work culture asks and answers on a unit-by-unit basis:

1. What do we want all students to know and be able to do? (The essential learning standards)

2. How will we know if they know it? (The assessment instruments and tasks teams use)

3. How will we respond if they don't know it? (Formative assessment processes for intervention)

4. How will we respond if they do know it? (Formative assessment processes for extension and enrichment)

The unit or chapter of content, then, becomes a natural cycle of time that is not too small (such as one week) and not too big (such as nine weeks) for meaningful analysis, reflection, and action by you and your teacher team throughout the year as you seek to answer the four critical questions of a PLC. A unit should be analyzed based on content standard clusters—that is, three to five essential standards (or sometimes a cluster of standards) for the unit. Thus, a teacher team, an administrative team, or a district office team does this type of analysis about eight to ten times per year.

This Mathematics at Work handbook consists of three chapters that fit the natural rhythm of your ongoing work as a teacher of mathematics and as part of a teacher team. The chapters bring a focus to ten high-leverage team actions (HLTAs) your team takes before, during, and in the immediate aftermath of a unit of instruction as you respond to the four critical questions of a PLC throughout the year, as highlighted in the previous feature box. Figure I.1 (page 4) lists the ten high-leverage team actions within their time frame in relation to the unit of instruction (before, during, or after) and then links the actions to the critical questions of a PLC that they address.

High-Leverage Team Actions	1. What do we want all students to know and be able to do?	2. How will we know if they know it?	3. How will we respond if they don't know it?	4. How will we respond if they do know it?
Before-the-Unit Team Actions				
HLTA 1. Making sense of the agreed-on essential learning standards (content and practices) and pacing	▉			
HLTA 2. Identifying higher-level-cognitive-demand mathematical tasks	▉	◧		
HLTA 3. Developing common assessment instruments	◧	▉		
HLTA 4. Developing scoring rubrics and proficiency expectations for the common assessment instruments		◧		
HLTA 5. Planning and using common homework assignments	◧	▉	◧	◧
During-the-Unit Team Actions				
HLTA 6. Using higher-level-cognitive-demand mathematical tasks effectively	◧	▉		
HLTA 7. Using in-class formative assessment processes effectively	◧		▉	▉
HLTA 8. Using a lesson-design process for lesson planning and collective team inquiry	▉	▉	▉	▉
After-the-Unit Team Actions				
HLTA 9. Ensuring evidence-based student goal setting and action for the next unit of study			▉	▉
HLTA 10. Ensuring evidence-based adult goal setting and action for the next unit of study			▉	▉

▉ = Fully addressed with high-leverage team action

◧ = Partially addressed with high-leverage team action

Figure I.1: High-leverage team actions aligned to the four critical questions of a PLC.

Visit **go.solution-tree.com/mathematicsatwork** to download a reproducible version of this figure.

Before the Unit

In chapter 1, we provide insight into the work of your collaborative team *before* the unit begins, along with the tools you will need in this phase. Your collaborative team expectation should be (as best you can) to complete this teaching and assessing work in preparation for the unit.

There are five before-the-unit high-leverage team actions for collaborative team agreement on a unit-by-unit basis.

> HLTA 1. Making sense of the agreed-on essential learning standards (content and practices) and pacing
>
> HLTA 2. Identifying higher-level-cognitive-demand mathematical tasks
>
> HLTA 3. Developing common assessment instruments
>
> HLTA 4. Developing scoring rubrics and proficiency expectations for the common assessment instruments
>
> HLTA 5. Planning and using common homework assignments

Once your team has taken these action steps, the mathematics unit begins.

During the Unit

In chapter 2, we provide the tools for and insight into the formative assessment work of your collaborative team *during* the unit. This chapter teaches deeper understanding of content, discussing Mathematical Practices and processes and using higher-level-cognitive-demand mathematical tasks effectively. It helps your team with daily lesson design and study ideas as ongoing in-class student assessment becomes part of a teacher-led formative process.

This chapter introduces three during-the-unit high-leverage team actions your team works through on a unit-by-unit basis.

> HLTA 6. Using higher-level-cognitive-demand mathematical tasks effectively
>
> HLTA 7. Using in-class formative assessment processes effectively
>
> HLTA 8. Using a lesson-design process for lesson planning and collective team inquiry

The end of each unit results in some type of student assessment. You pass back the assessments scored and with feedback. Then what? What are students to do? What are you to do?

After the Unit

In chapter 3, we provide tools for and insight into the formative work your collaborative team does *after* the unit is over. After students have taken the common assessment, they are expected to reflect on the results of their work and use the common unit assessment instrument for formative feedback purposes.

In addition, there is another primary formative purpose to using a common end-of-unit assessment, which Hattie (2012) describes in *Visible Learning for Teachers*: "This [teachers collaborating] is not critical reflection, but *critical reflection in light of evidence* about their teaching" (p. 19, emphasis added).

From a practical point of view, an end-of-unit analysis of the common assessment focuses your team's next steps for teaching and assessing for the next unit. Thus, there are two end-of-unit high-leverage team actions your team works through on a unit-by-unit basis.

> HLTA 9. Ensuring evidence-based student goal setting and action for the next unit of study
>
> HLTA 10. Ensuring evidence-based adult goal setting and action for the next unit of study

In *Principles to Actions: Ensuring Mathematical Success for All*, NCTM (2014) presents a modern-day view of professional development for mathematics teachers: building the knowledge capacity of every teacher. More importantly, however, you and your colleagues should intentionally *act* on that knowledge and transfer what you learn into daily classroom practice through the ten high-leverage teacher team actions presented in this handbook. For more information on the connection between these two documents, see appendix D on page 157.

Although given less attention, the difficult work of collective inquiry and action orientation has a more direct impact on student learning than when you work in isolation (Hattie, 2009). Through your team commitment (the engine that drives the PLC at Work culture and processes of collective inquiry and action research), you will find meaning in the collaborative work with your colleagues.

In *Great by Choice*, Jim Collins (2011) asks, "Do we really believe that our actions count for little, that those who create something great are merely lucky, that our circumstances imprison us?" He then answers, "Our research stands firmly against this view. Greatness is not primarily a matter of circumstance; greatness is first and foremost a matter of conscious choice and discipline" (p. 181). We hope this handbook helps you focus your time, energy, choices, and pursuit of a great teaching journey.

CHAPTER 1

Before the Unit

Teacher: Know thy impact.

—John Hattie

The ultimate outcome of planning before the unit begins is for you and your team members to gain a clear understanding of the impact of your expectations for student learning and demonstrations of understanding during the unit.

In conjunction with the scope and sequence your district mathematics curriculum provides, your collaborative team prepares a roadmap that describes what students will know and be able to demonstrate at the conclusion of the unit. To create this roadmap, your collaborative team prepares and organizes your work around five before-the-unit-begins high-leverage team actions.

HLTA 1. Making sense of the agreed-on essential learning standards (content and practices) and pacing

HLTA 2. Identifying higher-level-cognitive-demand mathematical tasks

HLTA 3. Developing common assessment instruments

HLTA 4. Developing scoring rubrics and proficiency expectations for the common assessment instruments

HLTA 5. Planning and using common homework assignments

These five team pursuits are based on step one of the PLC teaching-assessing-learning cycle (Kanold, Kanold, & Larson, 2012) shown in figure 1.1 (page 8). This cycle drives your pursuit of a meaningful formative assessment and learning process for your team and for your students throughout the unit and the year.

In this chapter, we describe each of the five before-the-unit-begins high-leverage team actions in more detail (the what) along with suggestions for how to achieve these pursuits (the how). Each HLTA section ends with an opportunity for you to evaluate your current reality (your team progress). The chapter ends with time for reflection and action (setting your Mathematics at Work priorities for team action).

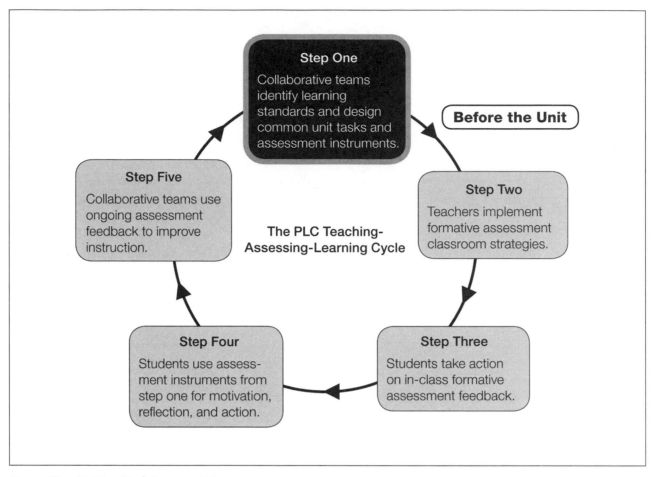

Source: Kanold, Kanold, & Larson, 2012.

Figure 1.1: Step one of the PLC teaching-assessing-learning cycle.

HLTA 1: Making Sense of the Agreed-On Essential Learning Standards (Content and Practices) and Pacing

An excellent mathematics program includes curriculum that develops important mathematics along coherent learning progressions and develops connections among areas of mathematical study and between mathematics and the real world.

—Steven Leinwand, Daniel J. Brahier, DeAnn Huinker,
Robert Q. Berry III, Frederick L. Dillon, et al.

In most K–5 grade levels, there will be eight to ten mathematics units (or chapters) during the school year. These units may also consist of several learning modules depending on how your curriculum is structured. An ongoing challenge is for you and your team to determine how to best make sense of and develop understanding for each of the agreed-on essential learning standards within the mathematics unit.

The What

Recall there are four critical questions every collaborative team in a PLC asks and answers on an ongoing unit-by-unit basis.

1. What do we want all students to know and be able to do? (The essential learning standards)

2. How will we know if they know it? (The assessment instruments and tasks teams use)

3. How will we respond if they don't know it? (Formative assessment processes for intervention)

4. How will we respond if they do know it? (Formative assessment processes for extension and enrichment)

High-Leverage Team Action	1. What do we want all students to know and be able to do?	2. How will we know if they know it?	3. How will we respond if they don't know it?	4. How will we respond if they do know it?
Before-the-Unit Action				
HLTA 1. Making sense of the agreed-on essential learning standards (content and practices) and pacing	▨			

▨ = Fully addressed with high-leverage team action

This first high-leverage team action enhances clarity on the first PLC critical question for collaborative team learning: What do we want all students to know and be able to do? The essential learning standards for the unit—the guaranteed and viable mathematics curriculum—include what (clusters and standards) students will learn, when they will learn it (the pacing of the unit), and how they will learn it (often via standards such as the Common Core Standards for Mathematical Practice). The Standards for Mathematical Practice "describe varieties of expertise that mathematic educators at all levels should seek to develop in their students" (National Governors Association Center for Best Practices [NGA] & Council of Chief State School Officers [CCSSO], 2010, p. 6). Following are the eight Standards for Mathematical Practice, which we include in full in appendix A (page 149).

1. Make sense of problems and persevere in solving them.
2. Reason abstractly and quantitatively.
3. Construct viable arguments and critique the reasoning of others.
4. Model with mathematics.
5. Use appropriate tools strategically.
6. Attend to precision.
7. Look for and make use of structure.
8. Look for and express regularity in repeated reasoning. (NGA & CCSSO, 2010, pp. 6–8)

While different school districts use many names for learning standards—*learning goals*, *learning targets*, *learning objectives*, and so on—this handbook references the broad mathematical concepts and understandings for the entire unit as *essential learning standards*. For more specific lesson-by-lesson daily outcomes, we use *daily learning objectives* or *essential questions*. We use the terms *learning goals* or *learning targets* to reference the outcome for student proficiency in each standard. The daily learning objectives and the tasks and activities representing those objectives help students understand the essential learning standards for the unit in order to demonstrate proficiency (outcomes) on these standards. The daily learning objectives articulate for students what they are to learn *that day* and at the same time provide insight for teachers on how to assess students on the essential learning standards at the end of the unit.

A unit of instruction connects topics in mathematics that are naturally grouped together—the essential ideas or content standard clusters. Each unit should consist of about four to six essential learning standards taught to every student in the course. These essential learning standards may consist of several daily learning objectives, sometimes described as the essential questions that support your daily lessons. The *context* of the lesson is the driving force for the entire lesson-design process. Each lesson context centers on clarity of the mathematical content and the processes for student learning.

The crux of any successful mathematics lesson rests on your collaborative team identifying and determining the daily learning objectives that align with the essential learning standards for the unit. Although you might develop daily learning objectives for each lesson as part of curriculum writing or review, your collaborative team should take time during lesson-design discussions to make sense of the essential learning standards for the unit and to consider how they are connected. This involves unpacking the mathematics content as well as the Mathematical Practices or processes each student will engage in as he or she learns the mathematics of the unit. *Unpacking*, in this case, means making sense of the mathematics listed in the standard, making sense of how the content connects to content learned in other grades as well as within the grade, and making sense of how students might develop both conceptual understanding and procedural skill with the mathematics listed in the standard.

The How

As you and your collaborative team unpack the mathematics content standards (the essential learning standards) for the unit, it is also important to decide which Standards for Mathematical Practice (or process) will receive focused development throughout the unit of instruction.

Unpacking a Learning Standard

How can your team explore the general unpacking of content and linking the content to student Mathematical Practices for any unit? Consider the third-grade mathematics content standard cluster *Understand properties of multiplication and the relationship between multiplication and division* in the domain Operations and Algebraic Thinking (3.OA). This content standard cluster consists of two standards: "Apply properties of operations as strategies to multiply and divide" and "Understand division as an unknown-factor problem" (NGA & CCSSO, 2010, p. 23). For the purpose of this discussion, focus your understanding on how to apply strategies based on properties of operations to multiply. See also the CCSS website (www.corestandards.org) to explore the Mathematical Practices and standards.

You can use the discussion questions from figure 1.2 to discuss an appropriate learning process you and your collaborative team could create for applying strategies to multiply.

Directions: Within your collaborative team, answer the following questions that address strategies to multiply.

1. What does it mean to apply strategies based on properties of operations to multiply?

2. How might students engage in the process of applying strategies to multiply?

3. Which Mathematical Practices should we highlight during a unit focused on applying strategies based on properties of operations to multiply?

Figure 1.2: Sample essential learning standard discussion tool.

Visit **go.solution-tree.com/mathematicsatwork** to download a reproducible version of this figure.

Think about how you would expect students to demonstrate their understanding of both the standard of using properties correctly and Mathematical Practice 7, "Look for and make use of structure."

Share your property-based strategies to find 6 × 7 with your team members, and discuss which properties you used to find the product. For example, you may have created a web to illustrate the properties you used (such as figure 1.3, page 12). Once your team brainstorms various strategies, focus your team discussion on the connection between the strategies and properties of operations.

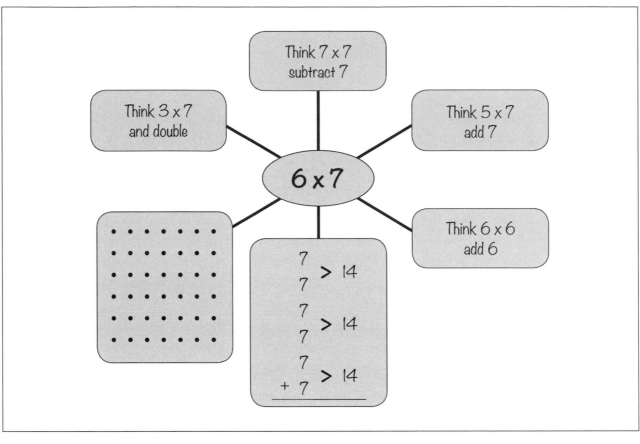

Figure 1.3: Strategies for finding 6 × 7.

Your collaborative team's conversation might have been similar to what follows: "What strategies can we use to find 6 × 7?" One collaborative team member might say, "I think of 6 × 7 as 3 × 7, and then I double that product." Another might use the break-apart strategy and say, "I break apart the 6, and I think 5 × 7, and then I add 7." The team should continue in this manner sharing strategies for 6 × 7. Eventually, the conversation will need to connect strategies to properties of operations if all students are to achieve the learning standard.

The team should identify properties including the commutative property, associative property, and distributive property. How can your team apply those properties to support the strategies identified for 6 × 7? Exploration of the mathematics standards at this grain size is crucial for making sense of the learning standards and should take place in the collaborative team setting. Team members must feel comfortable exploring the mathematics they will teach and discussing uncertainties within the collaborative team.

This is especially important since you or your colleagues were not necessarily taught the way you are expected to teach using various strategies that develop understanding. For example, a team member might not know what property connects to the doubling strategy in figure 1.3. Others on your team should help this teacher understand how the associative property supports this strategy because the teacher is thinking of the 6 as 2 × 3 and rather than thinking about (2 × 3) × 7, the teacher is using the strategy 2 × (3 × 7).

Similarly, the team can connect the distributive property to the break-apart strategy we described earlier. Together you might see that when using the break-apart strategy to think of 6 as 5 + 1, students have 6 × 7 = (5 + 1) × 7, and they are using the distributive property to multiply 5 × 7 then adding 1 × 7, because 6 × 7 = (5 + 1) × 7 = (5 × 7) + (1 × 7).

This level of unpacking of the essential learning standards is crucial *before* you can plan for effective student engagement with the mathematics. For example, once you make sense of how to use the properties of operations as strategies to multiply, it might become more clear that students could engage in Mathematical Practice 7, "Look for and make use of structure," to explore how strategies based on properties of operations can help when multiplying.

You might also observe an application of Mathematical Practice 8, "Look for and express regularity in repeated reasoning," when planning opportunities for students to use the doubling strategy to solve multiplication problems that have even factors by providing several examples where that strategy is useful.

Unpacking a Unit

The key elements of this first high-leverage team action are making sense of the essential learning standards, planning for student engagement in the Mathematical Practices or processes that support them, and deciding on common pacing for the unit. These elements need to occur before the unit begins in order to take full advantage of instructional time during the unit. In the case of the content standard cluster *Understand properties of multiplication and the relationship between multiplication and division* in the domain 3.OA, without teacher team focus on unpacking the learning standard, students might not be urged to move past drawing pictures of groups of objects to multiply. Instruction might be limited to moving directly from drawing pictures of groups to memorizing basic multiplication facts. Both of these options do not meet the learning standard "Apply properties of operations as strategies to multiply."

Your collaborative team may need to use outside resources to make sense of the mathematics involved in the unit. The background information in your school textbook teacher's edition and digital resources can be a good source for this foundational knowledge, as can resources from the National Council of Teachers of Mathematics (www.nctm.org), such as the *Essential Understanding* series.

In general, your team can use figure 1.4 (page 14) as a planning discussion tool to help you better understand the essential learning standards in each of your grade-level units.

Thus, unpacking your own understanding of the essential learning standards, narrowing the more specific daily learning objectives, and identifying appropriate Mathematical Practices and processes to support those standards are crucial steps to providing a clear path to impact student learning. This will ensure your students will benefit from opportunities for deeper understanding during the unit.

Consider the sample unit plan for grade 3 in figure 1.5 (pages 15–17) to help students develop strategies based on properties of operations to multiply (supportive of domain 3.OA and essential learning standard 3.OA.5).

Directions: Discuss the following prompts or questions with your collaborative teams to unpack essential learning standards, the prerequisite skills for the unit, the associated Mathematical Practices relevant to the current unit of study for your grade level, and the pacing decisions for the unit.

1. List the agreed-on essential learning standards for this unit.

2. What is the prerequisite knowledge needed to engage students with the essential learning standards?

3. What is the time frame available to teach this unit, and how will that time be distributed for each essential learning standard?

4. What are the mathematics vocabulary and literacy skills necessary for student success in this unit?

5. What are specific teaching strategies we can use to most effectively teach each essential learning standard for the unit? (See the example in figure 1.3, page 12.)

6. Which Mathematical Practices or processes should we highlight during the unit in order to better engage students in the process of understanding each essential learning standard?

Figure 1.4: Discussion tool for making sense of the agreed-on essential learning standards for the unit.

Visit **go.solution-tree.com/mathematicsatwork** to download a reproducible version of this figure.

Unit Name: Multiplication Facts and Strategies	Unit Number: 4
Standard **3.OA.B.5:** Apply properties of operations as strategies to multiply and divide.* Examples: If 6 × 4 = 24 is known, then 4 × 6 = 24 is also known (commutative property of multiplication). 3 × 5 × 2 can be found by 3 × 5 = 15, then 15 × 2 = 30, or by 5 × 2 = 10, then 3 × 10 = 30 (associative property of multiplication). Knowing that 8 × 5 = 40 and 8 × 2 = 16, one can find 8 × 7 as 8 × (5 + 2) = (8 × 5) + (8 × 2) = 40 + 16 = 56 (distributive property).	**Mathematical Practices** • **Mathematical Practice 3:** "Construct viable arguments and critique the reasoning of others." • **Mathematical Practice 4:** "Model with mathematics." • **Mathematical Practice 7:** "Look for and make use of structure." • **Mathematical Practice 8:** "Look for and express regularity in repeated reasoning."
Time Frame 4–1 to 4–13	**Purpose** This unit develops the concept of using strategies based on properties of operations (such as the commutative, associative, and distributive properties) to multiply basic facts. Strategies to focus on: • Doubling strategy • Changing order of factors • Break-apart strategy
Overview of the Essential Learning Standards I can use the doubling strategy to multiply. I can change the order of factors to use facts I know to multiply. I can use the break-apart strategy to multiply. I can represent multiplication strategies with equations.	**Enduring Understanding and Essential Questions** How can you choose appropriate strategies based on properties of operations to multiply?

Prior Knowledge (What Knowledge and Skills Need to Be Spiraled?)
• Prerequisites for this unit are: • Represent multiplication as groups of objects   • Represent multiplication with concrete objects   • Connect multiplication to repeated addition

Key Vocabulary
• array   • factor   • product   • even   • odd   • equation

Assessment Evidence
• Mathematics journal prompts   • Classroom discourse   • Independent practice   • + Assessment 4–7: Using doubling and the commutative property   • + Assessment 4–13: Using doubling, the commutative property, and the break-apart strategy

Figure 1.5: Sample unit plan progression of content for applying properties of operations as strategies to multiply for grade 3.

continued →

Learning Plan (Unit Description)	Suggested Teaching Strategies, Procedures, and Notes to Teachers (For example, How will prior knowledge be addressed? When will assessments be used?)
Day 1	**Topic:** Multiply with 2. **Doubling facts:** Solve problems with a 2 as the first factor by doubling, such as 2×6 by thinking $6 + 6$. **Mathematical Practice 8:** Students explore many examples of facts with 2 as the first factor and notice that in each case, they can solve the facts by adding the second factor to itself, thus doubling the second factor. **Essential learning standard 1:** I can use the doubling strategy to multiply by 2. (3.OA.5)
Day 2	**Topic:** Multiply with 4. **Doubling doubles:** Solve problems with 4 as the first factor by first solving the double and then multiplying that product by 2. For example, 4×6 becomes $2 \times (2 \times 6)$. Students think 2×6 then double. **Mathematical Practice 3:** Students are challenged to apply the doubling strategy to facts with 4 as the first factor. The goal is for students to conjecture that they are doubling a double. Students must express their thinking and make sense of the thinking of others. **Essential learning standard 1:** I can multiply by 4 by doubling the product of multiplying by 2. (3.OA.5)
Days 3 and 4	**Topic:** Use doubles to multiply with 6 and 8. **Extending doubles:** Extend doubling strategy to all facts with an even first factor. For example, 6×7 becomes $2 \times (3 \times 7)$. Make the connection to the associative property explicit. **Mathematical Practice 7:** Students see that all even numbers can be described as $2 \times n$. Once they identify this structure, students apply the doubling strategy to all facts with even first factors. **Essential learning standard 1:** I can use the doubling strategy to multiply by even factors. (3.OA.5)
Day 5	**Topic:** Model with arrays. **Modeling the commutative property:** Prepare for making sense of the commutative property by modeling products with arrays. **Mathematical Practice 8:** Students use arrays to represent several facts and see that facts in the form of $a \times b$ have the same product as facts in the form of $b \times a$. Students see that the columns and rows are just interchanged, leaving the same number of total objects in the array. **Essential learning standard 2:** I can use an array to represent multiplication. (3.OA.5)
Day 6	**Topic:** Use the commutative property. **Using the commutative property:** Make sense of the commutative property through the use of arrays so that students can use the doubling strategy with factors that have an odd first factor and an even second factor. For example, $7 \times 6 = 6 \times 7$, so the fact can be solved using the doubling strategy. **Mathematical Practice 8:** Students use arrays to represent several facts and see that facts in the form of $a \times b$ have the same product as facts in the form of $b \times a$. They see that the columns and rows are just interchanged, leaving the same number of total objects in the array. **Essential learning standard 2:** I can change the order of factors to use facts I know to multiply.

Day 7	**Assessment 4–7:** Use doubling and the commutative property.
Day 8	**Topic:** Multiply with 5.
	Apply the commutative property and skip counting to multiply with 5.
	Essential learning standard 2: I can change the order of factors and use skip counting to multiply with 5.
Day 9	**Topic:** Break apart numbers to multiply.
	Using the distributive property: Derive the product of facts from known facts by using the break-apart strategy. For example, solve 6 × 7 by using arrays to see that you can solve 6 × 7 by thinking 5 × 7 then add 7.
	Mathematical Practice 7: Students use arrays to see that they can find parts of arrays and combine them to determine the total number of objects in the arrays.
	Essential learning standard 3: I can use the break-apart strategy with facts I know to multiply.
Day 10	**Topic:** Multiply with 3 and 6.
	Apply the break-apart strategy and the commutative strategy to find products of facts with factors of 3 or 6.
	Mathematical Practice 7: Students use arrays to see that they can find parts of arrays and combine them to determine the total number of objects in the arrays.
	Essential learning standard 3: I can use the break-apart strategy and change the order of factors to multiply.
Day 11	**Topic:** Multiply with 7 and 9.
	Apply the break-apart strategy and the commutative strategy to find products of facts with factors of 3 or 6.
	Mathematical Practice 7: Students use arrays to see that they can find parts of arrays and combine them to determine the total number of objects in the arrays.
	Essential learning standard 3: I can use the break-apart strategy with facts I know to multiply.
Day 12	**Topic:** Use the associative and distributive properties (algebra).
	Connect the break-apart strategy to the distributive property by showing that 6 × 7 is really (5 + 1) × 7 and equals (5 × 7) + (1 × 7).
	Mathematical Practice 4: Students use the array they explored with the break-apart strategy to write expressions to represent the partial products.
	Essential learning standard 4: I can represent multiplication strategies with equations.
Day 13	**Assessment 4–13:** Use doubling, the commutative property, and the break-apart strategy.

Differentiation	
Enhancement	**Remediation**
Students write word problems to match a given expression and then apply strategies to multiply.	Students use concrete materials to represent properties of operations.
Students explore multiple strategies for the same fact, providing justification for which strategy is most efficient.	Students apply properties of operations as strategies using facts with lesser factors.
Resources	**Technology**
• Two-color counters	None
• Grid paper	

While some Mathematical Practices are pervasive throughout the unit, such as Mathematical Practice 3, it is important to target specific practices for planning purposes.

Source for standards: NGA & CCSSO, 2010, pp. 6–8, 23.

Visit **go.solution-tree.com/mathematicsatwork** to download reproducible versions of this figure.

Notice how figure 1.5 also provides guidance for the common pacing expectations of the unit. While unpacking the essential learning standards, your team will need to reach agreement on the total number of days needed for the unit, the expected date for the end-of-unit assessment, and the timing of your review for student performance on the end-of-unit assessment (discussed further in chapter 3, page 121).

Your Team's Progress

It is helpful to diagnose your team's current reality and action prior to launching the unit. Ask each team member to individually assess your team on the first high-leverage team action using the status check tool in table 1.1. Discuss your perception of your team's progress on making sense of the agreed-on essential learning standards and pacing. It matters less which stage your team is at and more that you and your team members are committed to working together to focus on understanding the learning standards and the best activities and strategies for increasing student understanding and achievement as your team seeks stage IV—sustaining.

Table 1.1: Before-the-Unit Status Check Tool for HLTA 1—Making Sense of the Agreed-On Essential Learning Standards (Content and Practices) and Pacing

Directions: Discuss your perception of your team's progress on the first high-leverage team action—making sense of the agreed-on essential learning standards (content and practices) and pacing. Defend your reasoning.			
Stage I: Pre-Initiating	**Stage II: Initiating**	**Stage III: Developing**	**Stage IV: Sustaining**
We do not discuss the essential learning standards of the unit prior to teaching it.	We discuss and reach agreement on the four to six essential learning standards for the unit.	We unpack the intent of each essential learning standard for the unit and discuss daily learning objectives to achieve each essential standard.	We connect the four to six essential learning standards to the Mathematical Practices before the unit begins.
We do not know which essential learning standards other colleagues of the same course or grade level teach during the unit.	We discuss and share how to develop student understanding of the essential learning standards during the unit.	We collaborate with our colleagues to make informed decisions about instruction of the essential learning standards for each lesson in the unit.	We have procedures in place to review the effectiveness of the students' roles, activities, experiences, and success on the essential learning standards during the unit.
We do not discuss lesson tasks.	We connect and align some lesson tasks to the essential learning standards for the unit.	We share effective teaching strategies for the essential learning standards of the unit.	We have procedures in place that ensure our team aligns the most effective mathematical tasks and instructional strategies to the content progression established in our overall unit plan components.
We do not discuss the Mathematical Practices as part of our unit planning.	We discuss the Mathematical Practices that best align to the essential learning standards for the unit.	We agree on the Mathematical Practices that best align to the learning standards for the unit.	We implement the Mathematical Practices that best align to the learning standards for the unit.

Visit **go.solution-tree.com/mathematicsatwork** to download a reproducible version of this table.

Your responses to table 1.1 will help you determine what you and your team are doing well with respect to your focus on essential learning standards and where you might need to place more attention before the unit begins.

Once your team unpacks and understands the essential learning standards you are ready to identify and prepare for higher-level-cognitive-demand mathematical tasks related to those essential learning standards. It is necessary to include tasks at varying levels of demand during instruction. The idea is to match the tasks and their cognitive demand to the essential learning standard expectations for the unit. Selecting mathematical tasks together is the topic of the second high-leverage team action, HLTA 2.

HLTA 2: Identifying Higher-Level-Cognitive-Demand Mathematical Tasks

The function of education is to teach one to think intensively and to think critically.

—Martin Luther King Jr.

Developing your team's understanding of the essential learning standards for the unit helped you answer the first critical question of a PLC, What do we want all students to know and be able to do? The mathematical tasks you and your team choose to use every day during the unit help you answer this first critical question as well.

The mathematical tasks you choose each day and for every unit also partially answer the second critical question of a PLC, How will we know if they know it?

High-Leverage Team Action	1. What do we want all students to know and be able to do?	2. How will we know if they know it?	3. How will we respond if they don't know it?	4. How will we respond if they do know it?
Before-the-Unit Action				
HLTA 2. Identifying higher-level-cognitive-demand mathematical tasks	▨	▨▢		

▨ = Fully addressed with high-leverage team action

▨▢ = Partially addressed with high-leverage team action

The What

What is a mathematical task?

NCTM first identified *mathematical task* in its *Professional Teaching Standards* (1991, 2008) as "worthwhile mathematical tasks" (p. 24). Melissa Boston and Peg Smith (2009) later provided this succinct definition: "A mathematical task is a single complex problem or a set of problems that focuses students' attention on a specific mathematical idea" (p. 136).

Mathematical tasks include activities, examples, or problems to complete as a whole class, in small groups, or individually. The tasks provide the rigor (levels of complex reasoning as provided by the conceptual understanding, procedural fluency, and application of the tasks) that students require and thus become an essential aspect of your team's collaboration and discussion. In short, the tasks are the problems you choose to determine the pathway of student learning and to assess student success along that pathway. As a teacher, you are empowered to decide what and how a student learns through your choice and use of mathematical tasks in class.

The type of instructional tasks you and your team select and use will determine students' opportunities to develop proficiency in Mathematical Practices and processes and will support the development of conceptual understanding and procedural skills for the essential learning standards. As Glenda Lappan and Diane Briars (1995) state:

> There is no decision that teachers make that has a greater impact on students' opportunities to learn and on their perceptions about what mathematics is than the selection or creation of the tasks with which the teacher engages students in studying mathematics. (p. 139)

Mathematical Practice 1—"Make sense of problems and persevere in solving them"—establishes the expectation for regularly engaging your students in challenging, higher-level-cognitive-demand mathematical tasks essential for their development. A growing body of research links students' engagement in higher-level-cognitive-demand mathematical tasks to overall increases in mathematics achievement, not just in the ability to solve problems (Hattie, 2012; Resnick, 2006).

A key collaborative team decision is which tasks to use in a particular lesson to help students attain the daily learning objective. The nature of the tasks with which your students engage provides the common student learning experiences you can draw on to further student learning at various points throughout the unit. Selecting appropriate tasks provides your collaborative team with the opportunity for rich, engaging, and professional discussions regarding expectations about student performance for the unit.

Thus, four critical task questions for your grade-level collaborative team to consider include:

1. What nature of tasks should we use for each essential learning standard of the unit? Will the tasks focus on building student conceptual understanding, procedural fluency, or a combination? Will the tasks involve application of concepts and skills?
2. What are the depth, rigor, order of presentation, and ways of investigating that we should use to ensure students learn the essential learning standards?
3. How does our collaborative team choose the mathematical tasks that best represent each essential learning standard?
4. How does our team ensure the implementation of the tasks as a team in order to avoid wide variances in student learning across the grade level?

Conceptual understanding *and* procedural fluency are essential aspects for students to become mathematically proficient. In light of this, the tasks you choose to form the unit's lessons must include a balance of higher- and lower-level-cognitive-demand expectations for students. Your team will also need to decide which mathematical tasks to use for class instruction and which tasks to use for the various assessment instruments given to students during and at the end of a unit.

Higher-level-cognitive-demand lessons or tasks are those that provide "opportunities for students to explain, describe, justify, compare, or assess; to make decisions and choices; to plan and formulate questions; to exhibit creativity; and to work with more than one representation in a meaningful way" (Silver, 2010, p. 2). In contrast, lessons or tasks with only lower-level cognitive demand are "characterized as opportunities for students to demonstrate routine applications of known procedures or to work with a complex assembly of routine subtasks or non-mathematical activities" (Silver, 2010, p. 2).

However, selecting a task with higher-level cognitive demand does not ensure that students will engage in rigorous mathematical activity (Jackson et al., 2013). The cognitive demand of a mathematical task is often lowered (perhaps unintentionally) during the implementation phase of the lesson (Stein, Remillard, & Smith, 2007). During the planning phase, your team should discuss how you will respond when students urge you to lower the cognitive demand of the task during the lesson. Avoiding cognitive decline during task implementation is discussed further in chapter 2 (page 71, HLTA 6).

Thus, your teacher team responds to several mathematical task questions before each unit begins:

1. How do we define and differentiate between higher-level-cognitive-demand *and* lower-level-cognitive-demand tasks for each essential standard of the unit?

2. How do we select common higher-level-cognitive-demand and lower-level-cognitive-demand tasks for each essential standard of the unit?

3. How do we create higher-level-cognitive-demand tasks from lower-level-cognitive-demand tasks for each essential standard of the unit?

4. How do we use and apply higher-level-cognitive-demand tasks for each essential standard during the unit?

5. How will we respond when students urge us to lower the cognitive demand of the task during the implementation phase of the lesson?

Visit **go.solution-tree.com/mathematicsatwork** to download these questions as a discussion tool.

The How

A critical step in selecting and planning a higher-level-cognitive-demand mathematical task is working the task before giving it to students. Working the task provides insight into the extent to which it will engage students in the intended mathematics concepts, skills, and Mathematical Practices and how students might struggle. Working the task with your team provides information about possible solution strategies or pathways that students might demonstrate.

Defining Higher-Level and Lower-Level-Cognitive-Demand Mathematical Tasks

You choose mathematical tasks for every lesson, every day. Take a moment to describe how you choose the daily tasks and examples that you use in class. Do you make those decisions by yourself, with members of your team, before the unit begins, or the night before you teach the lesson? Where do you locate and choose your mathematical tasks? From the textbook? Online? From your district resources?

And, most importantly, how would you describe the rigor of each task you choose for your students? Rigor is not whether a problem is considered hard. For example, "What is 6×7?" might be a hard problem for some, but it is not rigorous. *Rigor of a mathematical task* is defined in this handbook as the level and the complexity of reasoning required by the student during the task (Kanold, Briars, & Fennell, 2012). A more rigorous version of this same task might be something like, "Provide two different ways to solve 6×7 using facts you might know."

There are several ways to label the demand or rigor of a task; however, for the purposes of this handbook, tasks are classified as either lower-level cognitive demand or higher-level cognitive demand as defined by Smith and Stein (1998) in their *Task Analysis Guide* and printed in full as appendix B (page 153). *Lower-level-cognitive-demand tasks* are typically focused on memorization or on performing standard or rote procedures without attention to the properties that support those procedures (Smith & Stein, 2011).

Higher-level-cognitive-demand tasks are tasks for which students do not have a set of predetermined procedures to follow to reach resolution or, if the tasks involve procedures, they require that students provide the justification for why and how the procedures can be performed. Smith and Stein (2011) describe these procedures as "procedures with connections" (p. 16) as opposed to "procedures without connections," the designation they use for lower-level-cognitive-demand tasks that are not just based on memorization.

Thus, the level of cognitive demand of the mathematical tasks you choose each day can be viewed as either lower- or higher-level cognitive demand as shown in figure 1.6.

Lower-Level Cognitive Demand

Memorization: Requires eliciting information such as a fact, definition, term, or a simple procedure, as well as performing a simple algorithm or applying a formula.

Procedures without connections: Requires the engagement of some mental processing beyond a recall of information.

Higher-Level Cognitive Demand

Procedures with connections: Requires complex reasoning, planning, using evidence, and explanations of thinking.

Doing mathematics: Requires complex reasoning, planning, developing, and thinking most likely over an extended period of time.

Source: Smith & Stein, 2012.

Figure 1.6: Four categories of cognitive demand.

Visit **go.solution-tree.com/mathematicsatwork** to download a reproducible version of this figure.

You may or may not have been fully aware that every task you choose to use with your students each day is either a lower- or higher-level-cognitive-demand task. Lower-level-cognitive-demand tasks take less time in class, and do not require much complex reasoning by students. Their efficiency is appealing. They are much easier to manage in class as a general rule and easily serve direct instruction from the front of the room. The fact that the new state assessments intend to dramatically increase the task rigor compared to current state assessments (Herman & Linn, 2013) is additional motivation for you to increase the cognitive demand of the mathematical tasks you use during instruction and assessment.

The very nature of the mathematical content expectations requires your students to demonstrate *understanding*, and thus a shift to a *balanced* task approach during the unit—the use of both higher- and lower-level-cognitive-demand tasks. In most elementary school classrooms, this will require an increase in the use of higher-level-cognitive-demand tasks. Figure 1.7 (page 24) provides six mathematical tasks, one for each grade level from kindergarten through grade 5, along with an identifier for the content standard each supports. Use the discussion tool to examine the mathematical task that most closely relates to the grade-level responsibilities of your collaborative team, and then answer the questions at the end of the tool.

Each of the tasks in figure 1.7 is a higher-level-cognitive-demand mathematical task. What makes a task high cognitive demand? What might a lower-level-cognitive-demand mathematical task look like for the same essential learning standard?

The tasks in figure 1.7 (page 24) represent procedures with connections or problem solving. Notice that the kindergarten task ("Blake has a number of cubes that is 1 more than 15. Jessica has a number of cubes that is 1 less than 17. Who has more cubes? How do you know?") would not require higher-level cognitive demand for a student in grade 4 to solve. The task's demand is relative to the students who will engage with the task, and it is connected to a specific essential question and learning objective for the particular unit. However, tasks that are lower-level cognitive demand can still be connected to the same learning standards.

Directions: Determine a solution for the mathematical task that most closely relates to the grade-level responsibilities of your collaborative team, and then answer the questions at the end of the tool.

Task for Kindergarten (K.CC.6)

Blake has a number of cubes that is 1 more than 15. Jessica has a number of cubes that is 1 less than 17. Who has more cubes? How do you know?

Task for Grade 1 (1.G.3)

Calvin is at a birthday party where children will be sitting at tables. The chairs are already set up at each table. At one table, there are two chairs, and the mini birthday cake is cut in halves. At another table, there are four chairs, and a mini birthday cake of the same size is cut in fourths.

Calvin thinks that he will get the same amount of cake wherever he sits because he will get a piece of birthday cake no matter what. Tell if you agree or disagree, and say why.

Task for Grade 2 (2.NBT.5)

Alex was partway finished with a problem in mathematics class in which she needed to find 48 + 25 when it was time to leave for lunch. The teacher picked up her paper and was not sure if Alex was correct. Describe how Alex could be correct as well as the last step she still had to complete.

$$48 + 25$$
$$40 + 20 = 60$$
$$8 + 2 = 10$$
$$60 + 10 = 70$$

Task for Grade 3 (3.OA.4)

A student in your class is asked to solve 6 × 7 without drawing pictures. The student does not know the fact. Provide two different ways the student could use multiplication to solve the fact by using other facts the student might know.

Task for Grade 4 (4.OA.2)

Write four different story problems to correspond to the following expression: 46 ÷ 4. Each problem should lead to a different answer. The answers to the problems should be 11½, 12, 11, and 2. Do not use the words *estimate*, *about*, or *round* in your problems.

Task for Grade 5 (5.NF.4a and 5.NF.6)

Write a word problem for ⅔ × ¾, then use a visual model to solve it that is supportive of the context used in your word problem.

Questions for Each Task

1. How are your collaborative team members' responses the same? How do they differ?

2. How do these tasks support the essential learning standards of the unit?

3. With which Mathematical Practices or processes might students engage while solving these tasks?

Figure 1.7: Higher-level-cognitive-demand mathematical task discussion tool.

Visit **go.solution-tree.com/mathematicsatwork** to download a reproducible version of this figure.

Use figure 1.8 to work with your collaborative team to adapt the higher-level-cognitive-demand mathematical tasks from figure 1.7 to lower-level-cognitive-demand mathematical tasks.

Directions: Record a lower-level cognitive demand adaptation for each task presented in figure 1.7.
Task for Kindergarten (K.CC.6)
Task for Grade 1 (1.G.3)
Task for Grade 2 (2.NBT.5)
Task for Grade 3 (3.OA.4)
Task for Grade 4 (4.OA.2)
Task for Grade 5 (5.NF.4a and 5.NF.6)

Figure 1.8: Corresponding lower-level-cognitive-demand mathematical task-creation tool.

Visit **go.solution-tree.com/mathematicsatwork** to download a reproducible version of this figure.

Compare the lower-level-cognitive-demand mathematical tasks you created to the corresponding lower-level-cognitive-demand mathematical tasks in figure 1.9 (page 26). Then, work with your collaborative team to answer the questions in figure 1.9 and compare the two types of tasks for each grade level.

Directions: Record your responses as you compare the lower-level-cognitive-demand mathematical tasks you developed in figure 1.8 (page 25) with the lower-level-cognitive-demand mathematical tasks presented in this figure.

Task for Kindergarten (K.CC.6)

Make a cube tower that is 15 cubes tall. Make another cube tower that is 17 cubes tall. Which tower is greater, the 15-cube tower or the 17-cube tower?

Task for Grade 1 (1.G.3)

The pictures below show mini birthday cakes. If you really like birthday cake, would you prefer to have a half of the birthday cake or one-fourth of the birthday cake?

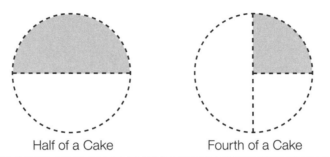

Half of a Cake   Fourth of a Cake

Task for Grade 2 (2.NBT.5)

Solve 48 + 25.

Task for Grade 3 (3.OA.4)

Solve 6 × 7.

Task for Grade 4 (4.OA.2)

There are 46 students going on a roller coaster during a field trip. Four students can go in each car. How many cars will be used if all of the students ride the roller coaster?

Task for Grade 5 (5.NF.4a and 5.NF.6)

Solve ⅔ × ¾.

Questions for Each Task

1. How do these tasks compare to the first set of tasks from figure 1.8?

2. What might you learn about your students through these tasks that is different from what you would learn using the figure 1.7 (page 24) tasks?

3. Which tasks are more closely representative of tasks you currently use with your students?

Figure 1.9: Comparing higher- and lower-level-cognitive-demand mathematical tasks.

Visit **go.solution-tree.com/mathematicsatwork** to download a reproducible version of this figure.

While lower-level-cognitive-demand mathematical tasks are crucial for developing procedural fluency, higher-level-cognitive-demand mathematical tasks are essential for improving students' depth of understanding related to the Common Core–type expectations and, ultimately, student achievement. You and your team should focus on creating tasks of varying cognitive demand in order to meet the expectations of your state assessments.

Identifying the Cognitive Demand of Your Mathematical Tasks

As a first step in understanding the nature of the current cognitive demand level of the tasks you use each day, use figure 1.10.

Name of the Unit:	
For at least two of the essential standards in this unit, provide samples of the types of mathematical tasks students will experience in class, for homework, or on assessments.	
Directions: Sort every task you use into the following four categories.	
Lower-Level Tasks	**Higher-Level Tasks**
Memorization	**Procedures With Connections**
Procedures Without Connections	**Doing Mathematics**

Figure 1.10: Tool for sorting unit tasks by cognitive demand level.

Visit **go.solution-tree.com/mathematicsatwork** to download a reproducible version of this figure.

What percentage of the current tasks you plan to use fall into the lower-level-cognitive-demand task category? What percentage fall into the higher-level-cognitive-demand task category? Do you have a proper balance in terms of the complexity of student reasoning required by the tasks you present to students throughout the unit?

Consider the grade 4 higher-level-cognitive-demand mathematical task from the Smarter Balanced Assessment Consortium (SBAC) in figure 1.11 (page 28) and the fractions task from the Partnership for Assessment of Readiness for College and Careers (PARCC) in figure 1.12 (page 28).

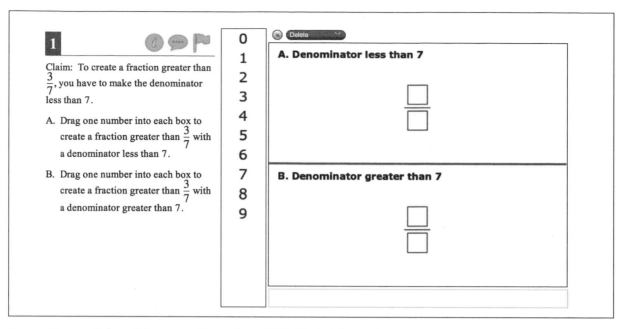

Source: Smarter Balanced Assessment Consortium, 2013. Used with permission.

Figure 1.11: Smarter Balanced Assessment Consortium practice test grade 4 task.

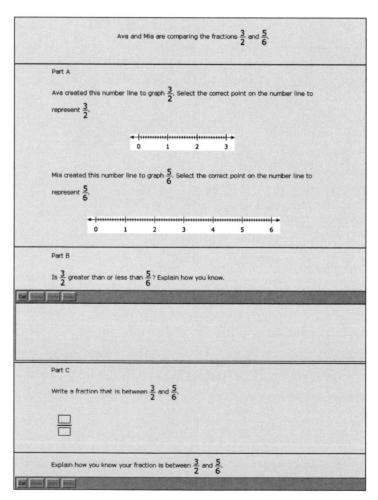

Source: PARCC, 2013.

Figure 1.12: PARCC practice test grade 4 task.

Using figures 1.11 and 1.12, explain where you would place these mathematical tasks in the cognitive demand table in figure 1.10 (page 27). You can also reference appendix B (page 153) for more detail. If you do believe these are higher-level-cognitive-demand tasks, explain why.

Visit **go.solution-tree.com/mathematicsatwork** for more higher-level-cognitive-demand mathematical tasks like these from the SBAC and PARCC assessments.

Creating Higher-Level-Cognitive-Demand Tasks

There are several strategies you can use to change a lower-level-cognitive-demand mathematical task to higher-level cognitive demand. A typical strategy that is rarely fruitful is to change the numbers in the problem to greater numbers. For example, with the grade 2 task in figure 1.9 (page 26), it would not be enough simply to change 48 + 25 to 148 + 325. While this might make a task more difficult to complete, it does not necessarily make the task higher-level cognitive demand. You can use the strategies in figure 1.13 to adjust a mathematical task from lower-level cognitive demand to higher-level cognitive demand.

- Rather than providing a context, ask students to write a word problem for a given expression.
- Have students determine an expression to represent a situation.
- Require students to provide justifications for their solutions.
- Challenge students to solve problems using more than one solution method or representation.
- Have students make sense of provided solution strategies by completing the solution or justifying the steps.
- Make the task open ended so that multiple responses will satisfy the task.
- Transform a single-step problem to a multiple-step problem.
- Include the use of multiple representations in a task.

Figure 1.13: Strategies for increasing the cognitive demand of tasks.

Visit **go.solution-tree.com/mathematicsatwork** to download a reproducible version of this figure.

Work with your grade-level collaborative team to create two tasks for the learning standards listed in figure 1.14 (page 30). One task should be higher-level cognitive demand, and the other should be lower-level cognitive demand. Provide a justification for your choices of tasks and cognitive level, and discuss with your team.

Directions: Write one lower- and one higher-level-cognitive-demand mathematical task for the essential learning standard presented for your grade level. Then, respond to the questions that follow.

Task for Grade K

Solve addition and subtraction word problems, and add and subtract within 10, such as by using objects or drawings to represent the problem. (K.OA.2)

Task for Grade 1

Use addition and subtraction within 20 to solve word problems involving situations of adding to, taking from, putting together, taking apart, and comparing with unknowns in all positions, such as by using objects, drawings, and equations with a symbol for the unknown number to represent the problem. (1.OA.1)

Task for Grade 2

Solve word problems involving dollar bills, quarters, dimes, nickels, and pennies, using $ and ¢ symbols appropriately. (2.MD.8)

---

continued →

Task for Grade 3

Compare two fractions with the same numerator or the same denominator by reasoning about their size. Recognize that comparisons are valid only when the two fractions refer to the same whole. Record the results of comparisons with the symbols >, =, and <, and justify the conclusions, such as by using a visual fraction model. (3.NF.3d)

Task for Grade 4

Solve word problems involving multiplication of a fraction by a whole number, such as by using visual fraction models and equations to represent the problem. (4.NF.4c)

Task for Grade 5

Find whole-number quotients of whole numbers with up to four-digit dividends and two-digit divisors, using strategies based on place value, the properties of operations, or the relationship between multiplication and division. Illustrate and explain the calculation by using equations, rectangular arrays, or area models. (5.NBT.6)

Questions for Each Task

1. How might what you learn about your students' understanding related to the learning standard differ depending on the demand of the task you use during instruction?

2. How did the strategies in figure 1.13 (page 29) help you to write higher-level-cognitive-demand mathematical tasks?

3. In what ways might you support the implementation of the higher-level-cognitive-demand mathematical tasks during instruction?

Source for standards: Adapted from NGA & CCSSO, 2010, pp. 11, 15, 20, 24, 30, 35.

Figure 1.14: Team discussion tool for identifying higher-level-cognitive-demand mathematical tasks for the unit.

Visit **go.solution-tree.com/mathematicsatwork** to download a reproducible version of this figure.

Once you include identifying the cognitive demand of mathematical tasks as part of your unit planning, your before-the-unit-begins activity will likely change. You will begin to look at tasks and classify them as higher-level or lower-level cognitive demand, and then decide the best timing during the unit and the lessons to use the higher-level-cognitive-demand mathematical tasks. Your goal should be to use a balance of both low and high during instruction and on the assessment instruments for the unit in order to pursue "conceptual understanding, procedural skills and fluency, and application with equal intensity" (Common Core State Standards Initiative, 2014, p. 1).

Preparing for the Use of Higher-Level-Cognitive-Demand Tasks

Before you use any higher-level-cognitive-demand task in class, your teacher team should:

1. Discuss your expectations for *student demonstration of quality work* (both successful and unsuccessful approaches) in defense of their mathematical argument for the task.

2. Discuss how your lesson plan for this problem *promotes student communication of their argument with others* and allows peer-to-peer–based solution defense.

To help your team facilitate this type of discussion, you can use figure 1.15 for any common higher-level-cognitive-demand task you might plan to use during the unit.

Directions: Use these questions to better understand how you will use any higher-level-cognitive-demand task in class.
What is the essential standard for the lesson? (What do you want students to know and understand about mathematics as a result of this lesson)?
In what ways does the task build on students' previous knowledge? What definitions, concepts, or ideas do students need to know to begin to work on this task? What prompts will you need to help students access their prior knowledge?
What are all the possible solution pathways for the task? Which of these pathways or strategies do you think students will use? What misconceptions might students have? What errors might students make?
What are the language demands of the task? How will you address these challenges if students are stuck during the task?
What are your expectations for students as they work on and complete this task? What tools or technology will they utilize to enhance student-to-student discourse?

Source: Adapted from Smith, Schwan, Bill, & Hughes, 2008.

Figure 1.15: Task analysis discussion tool.

Visit **go.solution-tree.com/mathematicsatwork** to download a reproducible version of this figure.

Your Team's Progress

It is helpful to diagnose your team's current reality and actions prior to launching the unit. Ask each team member to individually assess your team on the second high-leverage team action using the status check tool in table 1.2 (page 32). Discuss your perception of your team's progress on identifying higher-level-cognitive-demand mathematical tasks. It matters less which stage your team is at and more that you and your team members are committed to working together to focus on understanding the learning standards and the best activities and strategies for increasing student understanding and achievement as your team seeks stage IV—sustaining.

Your responses will help your team focus on the cognitive demand for your daily mathematical tasks and where you need to place more time and attention before the unit begins. Your intentional use of higher-level-cognitive-demand mathematical tasks will ensure students are aware of and developing deeper understanding of the learning standards.

Of course, using balanced cognitive demand tasks becomes an important feature of the common assessment instruments for the end of the unit as well. Creating and using common assessment instruments with a balance of cognitive demand across tasks for each learning standard is the next high-leverage team action.

Visit www.nctm.org or **go.solution-tree.com/mathematicsatwork** for more examples of grade level higher-level-cognitive-demand tasks and resources for those tasks.

Table 1.2: Before-the-Unit Status Check Tool for HLTA 2—Identifying Higher-Level-Cognitive-Demand Mathematical Tasks

Directions: Discuss your perception of your team's progress on the second high-leverage team action—identifying higher-level-cognitive-demand mathematical tasks. Defend your reasoning.			
Stage I: Pre-Initiating	**Stage II: Initiating**	**Stage III: Developing**	**Stage IV: Sustaining**
We do not discuss or share our use of the mathematical tasks in each unit of the curriculum.	We discuss and share some mathematical tasks we will use during the unit.	We explore and practice together mathematical tasks we will use during the unit.	We reach agreement on a collection of mathematical tasks every team member will use.
We do not share our understanding of the difference between lower- and higher-level-cognitive-demand mathematical tasks.	We do not base our instructional decisions and mathematical task choices on the cognitive demand of the task.	We are able to compare and contrast higher- and lower-level-cognitive-demand mathematical tasks for each learning standard of the unit.	We reach agreement on both the solution pathways for each mathematical task and the management of those tasks in the classroom.
We do not discuss the cognitive demand of the tasks we use in class.	We have reached agreement on what differentiates a higher- from a lower-level-cognitive-demand mathematical task.	We connect the mathematical tasks to the essential learning standards, daily lesson learning objectives, and corresponding activities for each unit.	We choose mathematical tasks that represent a balance of lower- and higher-level cognitive demand for the learning standards throughout the unit.
We do not use higher-level-cognitive-demand mathematical tasks.	We use higher-level-cognitive-demand mathematical tasks if they are included in the lesson.	We create higher-level-cognitive-demand mathematical tasks from lower-level-cognitive-demand mathematical tasks individually.	We create higher-level-cognitive-demand mathematical tasks from lower-level-cognitive-demand mathematical tasks as a team.

Visit **go.solution-tree.com/mathematicsatwork** to download a reproducible version of this table.

HLTA 3: Developing Common Assessment Instruments

One of the most powerful, high-leverage strategies for improving student learning is the creation of frequent, high-quality, common formative assessments.

—Richard DuFour, Rebecca DuFour, Robert Eaker, and Tom Many

Just as the mathematical tasks you and your teacher team choose for your lessons help you to partially answer the second critical question of a PLC—How will we know if they know it?—so do the choices your team makes for the during-the-unit and end-of-unit common assessment instruments.

As your team makes sense of the essential learning standards for the unit and better understands how to choose, adapt, and create higher-level-cognitive-demand mathematical tasks and learning activities, your team will be ready to develop common assessment instruments to assess students' understanding of the essential learning standards for the unit.

High-Leverage Team Action	1. What do we want all students to know and be able to do?	2. How will we know if they know it?	3. How will we respond if they don't know it?	4. How will we respond if they do know it?
Before-the-Unit Action				
HLTA 3. Developing common assessment instruments	◧	▣		

◼ = Fully addressed with high-leverage team action

◧ = Partially addressed with high-leverage team action

The What

Why is developing common assessment instruments an important before-the-unit-begins high-leverage activity? The process of creating common assessment instruments for each unit of your course supports learning conversations about prerequisite concepts and skills, common student errors, and ways of assessing students' understanding of the essential learning standards. It allows you to design lessons backward as you move from the outcomes (student demonstrations of knowledge on essential learning standards) for the unit to the learning activities, tasks, and resources students use during the unit and need for success on the end-of-unit assessments. Developing the common assessment instruments will also help you better prepare for using them for a formative process at the end of the unit. (This is discussed in detail in chapter 3 with HLTA 9, page 123.)

According to DuFour, DuFour, Eaker, and Many (2010):

> One of the most powerful, high-leverage strategies for improving student learning available to schools is the creation of frequent, high-quality, common formative assessments by teachers who are working collaboratively to help a group of students acquire agreed-upon knowledge and skills. (p. 75)

There is an important distinction between formative assessment *processes* your team uses and the assessment *instruments* used as part of those formative processes. James Popham (2011) provides an analogy to describe the difference between summative assessment instruments (such as your end-of-unit tests) and formative assessment processes (such as what you and your students *do* with those test results). He describes the difference between a surfboard and surfing.

> While a surfboard represents an important tool in surfing, it is only that—a part of the surfing process. The entire process involves the surfer paddling out to an appropriate offshore location, selecting the right wave, choosing the most propitious moment to catch the chosen wave, standing upright on the surfboard, and staying upright while a curling wave rumbles toward shore. (p. 36)

The surfboard is a key component of the surfing process, but it is not the entire process.

Your team's assessment instruments are the tools it uses to collect data about student demonstrations of the learning standards. The assessment instruments subsequently will inform you and your students' ongoing decisions about learning. Assessment instruments vary and can include such tools as class assignments, exit slips, quizzes, or unit tests; however, to avoid inequities in the level of rigor provided to students, and to serve the formative learning process, these assessment instruments must be *in common* for every teacher on your grade-level team.

When your collaborative team creates and adapts unit-by-unit common assessment instruments together, you enhance the focus and fidelity to student learning expectations across the grade level. The common assessment instruments can provide coherence by fostering learning progression continuity for students.

You minimize the wide variance in student task-performance expectations from teacher to teacher (an inequity creator) when you work collaboratively with colleagues to design high-quality assessment instruments appropriate to the identified essential learning standards for the unit.

The first questions your team must ask are, How do we know our end-of-unit assessments are of high quality? On what basis would we make these determinations?

The How

Collaborative teams consider the following when creating high-quality assessment instruments.

- What level of cognitive demand will we expect for each essential learning standard on the exam?

- What evidence of content knowledge will we assess for each essential learning standard?

- What evidence of student engagement in the Mathematical Practices will we assess for each essential learning standard?

- What types of question formats will we use to evaluate specific evidence of learning (such as multiple choice, short answer, multiple representations, explanation and justification, or using technology)?

Once your team decides the types of questions or tasks you will use to understand student thinking, your team will need to develop high-quality common assessment instruments that reflect those decisions and support student use of the assessment instrument as a learning tool.

Evaluating the Quality of Your Assessment Instruments

Your collaborative team can use figure 1.16 to evaluate the quality of your current assessment instruments, such as tests and quizzes, as well as to build new assessment instruments for the units.

Assessment Indicators	Description of Level 1	Requirements of the Indicator Are Not Present	Limited Requirements of This Indicator Are Present	Substantially Meets the Requirements of the Indicator	Fully Achieves the Requirements of the Indicator	Description of Level 4
Identification and emphasis on essential learning standards (specific feedback to students)	Learning standards are unclear and absent from the assessment instrument. Too much attention is given to one target.	1	2	3	4	Learning standards are clear, included on the assessment, and connected to the assessment questions.
Visual presentation	Assessment instrument is sloppy, disorganized, difficult to read, and offers no room for work.	1	2	3	4	Assessment is neat, organized, easy to read, and well-spaced, with room for teacher feedback.
Balance of higher- and lower-level-cognitive-demand tasks	Emphasis is on procedural knowledge with minimal higher-level-cognitive-demand tasks for demonstration of understanding.	1	2	3	4	Test is rigor balanced with higher-level and lower-level-cognitive-demand tasks present.
Clarity of directions	Directions are missing and unclear. Directions are confusing for students.	1	2	3	4	Directions are appropriate and clear.
Variety of assessment task formats	Assessment contains only one type of questioning strategy, and no multiple choice or evidence of the Mathematical Practices. Calculator usage not clear.	1	2	3	4	Assessment includes a blend of assessment types and assesses Mathematical Practices modeling or use of tools. Calculator expectations clear.
Tasks and vocabulary (attending to precision)	Wording is vague or misleading. Vocabulary and precision of language are a struggle for student understanding and access.	1	2	3	4	Vocabulary is direct, fair, accessible, and clearly understood by students, and they are expected to attend to precision in response.
Time allotment	Few students can complete the assessment in the time allowed.	1	2	3	4	Test can be successfully completed in the time allowed.
Appropriate scoring rubric (points)	Scoring rubric is not evident or is inappropriate for the assessment tasks presented.	1	2	3	4	Scoring rubric is clearly stated and appropriate for each task or problem.

Source: Adapted from Kanold, Kanold, and Larson, 2012, p. 94.

Figure 1.16: Assessment instrument quality-evaluation tool.

Visit **go.solution-tree.com/mathematicsatwork** to download a reproducible version of this figure.

Designing a High-Quality Assessment Instrument

Designing common assessment instruments before the unit provides a context for the discussion of prerequisite knowledge, which you may need to address during instruction while making sense of the essential learning standards. It also provides a context for discussing potential student errors or misconceptions.

Your collaborative team should rate and evaluate the quality of one of your most recent end-of-unit or chapter assessment instruments (tests) using the evaluation tool in figure 1.16 and figure 1.17 (pages 37–38), the High-Quality Assessment Diagnostic and Discussion Tool. How does it score—12? 16? 22? How close does your assessment instrument (your surfboard, so to speak) come to scoring a 27 or higher out of the 32 points possible in the rubric? It should be your expectation to write common assessment instruments that would score 4s in all eight categories of the assessment evaluation rubric.

Using figure 1.16, consider the third criteria—balance of cognitive demand. How did your collaborative team score? Was the assessment instrument you reviewed balanced according to procedurally and conceptually based tasks? Did you have a blend of higher- and lower-level cognitive demand questions?

Digging Into the Meaning of an Essential Learning Standard

Consider the Common Core grade 5 essential learning standard related to solving real-world problems involving division of unit fractions by nonzero whole numbers and division of whole numbers by unit fractions, such as by using visual fraction models and equations to represent the problem (5.NF.7c). First, what does this mean? It means that students need to solve word problems that represent problems like $3 \div \frac{1}{7}$ or $\frac{1}{3} \div 2$.

When asked to solve a problem like $3 \div \frac{1}{7}$, teachers typically think of changing 3 to $\frac{3}{1}$ and solving $\frac{3}{1} \times \frac{7}{1}$ while simultaneously reciting a silent chant that goes something like, "Stay, change, flip." This chant corresponds to the procedures most adults were taught to use to divide fractions. Many adults can determine the correct answer but have little understanding of how they were able to get it or why it makes sense.

For this learning standard, however, students need to use visual models to represent the problem. That becomes problematic because of how you tend to solve this type of problem by using multiplication. The problem is division, not multiplication. So what does $3 \div \frac{1}{7}$ mean? How could you represent this mathematical task visually? Understanding whole-number division aids fraction division. This learning standard is part of the content standard cluster *Understand properties of multiplication and the relationship between multiplication and division* in the domain Operations and Algebraic Thinking (3.OA): "Apply properties of operations as strategies to multiply and divide" and "Understand division as an unknown-factor problem" (NGA & CCSSO, 2010, p. 23). Therefore, a prerequisite to this task is an understanding of division of whole numbers.

In third grade, students divide whole numbers in context. They might be asked to solve $12 \div 4$ within a word problem. A common context for this problem is to share something, say cookies, equally among four friends. It is necessary but not sufficient for students in grade 3 to encounter problems like this. It is also necessary for students to encounter problems in which they measure out equal groups rather than share among groups equally. In this case, we would have twelve cookies and give four cookies to each friend to see how many friends will get cookies. The first word problem represents sharing or partitive division and the second measurement division. Which meaning will students use in fifth grade to represent $3 \div \frac{1}{7}$ in context?

Directions: Examine your most recent end-of-unit test and evaluate the quality of the test against the following eight criteria described in figure 1.16 (page 35).

1. Are the essential learning standards written on the test as student friendly and grade-appropriate "I can . . ." statements?

Discuss: What do your students think about learning mathematics? Do your students think learning mathematics is about doing a bunch of math problems? Or, can they explain the essential learning standards and perform on any task that might reflect that standard?

Note: In order for students to respond to the end-of-unit assessment feedback when it is passed back (HLTA 9, in chapter 3), this is a necessary test feature.

2. Does the visual presentation provide space for student work?

Discuss: Do your students have plenty of space to write out solution pathways, show their work, and explain their thinking for each task on the assessment instrument?

Note: This criterion often is one of the reasons not to use the written tests that come with your textbook series. You can use questions from the test bank aligned to your instruction, but space problems as needed.

3. Is there an appropriate balance of higher- and lower-level-cognitive-demand questions on the test?

Discuss: What percentage of all tasks or problems on the assessment instrument are of lower-level cognitive demand? What percentage are of higher-level cognitive demand? Is there an appropriate balance? Unless this has been a major focus of your work, your current end-of-unit tests may not score very high in this criterion.

Note: Use figure 1.15 (page 31) as a tool to determine rigor. This will help you to better understand the level of cognitive demand. Also, see page 42 at the end of this section for more advice on this criterion. As a good rule of thumb, rigor balance ratio should be about 30/70 (higher- to lower-level-cognitive demand) on the assessment.

4. Is there clarity with all directions?

Discuss: What does clarity mean to each member of our team? Are any of the directions for the different test questions or tasks confusing to the student? Why?

Note: The verbs (actions words) used in the directions for each set of tasks or problems are very important to notice when discussing clarity.

5. Is there variety in assessment formats?

Discuss: Does our test use a blend of assessment formats or types? Do we include questions that allow for technology as a tool, such as graphing calculators? Did we balance the use of different question formats? If we used multiple choice, did we include items with multiple possible answers similar to those on the PARCC, SBAC, or other state assessments?

Note: Your end-of-unit assessments should not be of either extreme: all multiple-choice or all open-ended questions.

continued →

6. Is the language both precise and accessible?

Discuss: Is the vocabulary for each task used on our end-of-unit assessment clear, accessible, and direct for students? Do we attend to the precision of language used during the unit, and do the students understand the language used on the assessment?

Note: Does the assessment instrument place the proper language supports needed for all students?

7. Is enough time allotted for students to complete the assessment?

Discuss: Can our students complete this assessment in the time allowed? What will be our procedure if they cannot complete the assessment within the allotted time?

Note: Each teacher on the team should complete a full solution key for the assessment as will be expected of students. For upper-level students, it works well to use a time ratio of 3:1 (or 4:1) for student to teacher completion time to estimate how long it will take students to complete an assessment. For elementary students, it may take much longer to complete the assessment. All teachers should use the agreed-upon time allotment.

8. Are our scoring rubrics clear and appropriate?

Discuss: Are the scoring rubrics to be used for every task clearly stated on the test? Do our scoring rubrics (total points for the test) make sense based on the complexity of reasoning for the task? Are the scoring points assigned to each task appropriate and agreed upon by each teacher on the team?

Note: See HLTA 4 (page 46) for more details.

Summary: Using your score from the figure 1.16 assessment tool (page 35), which specific aspects of your current unit assessment instruments need to be improved?

_____

_____

_____

_____

_____

_____

_____

_____

_____

_____

_____

_____

Figure 1.17: High-quality assessment diagnostic and discussion tool.

Visit **go.solution-tree.com/mathematicsatwork** to download a reproducible version of this figure.

Your students need to be assessed for dividing fractions in context. A good way to assess this through the use of a higher-level-cognitive-demand mathematical task is by asking students to actually write word problems (creating a context) to represent the operation. Students might be asked to write a word problem to represent $3 \div \frac{1}{7}$ and then use visual fraction models to determine the quotient.

If you use sharing division, you would have three cookies to share among $\frac{1}{7}$ of a friend—that does not make sense as one cannot have a *part* of a friend, and it will not work for this problem. However, using measurement division, we could begin with three cookies and give each friend $\frac{1}{7}$ of a cookie. The quotient would be the number of friends given cookies. How might we represent this visually? The visual model becomes clearer now that we have a problem context. We could draw three cookies and then divide each into sevenths to see how many sevenths we can make from three cookies (see figure 1.18).

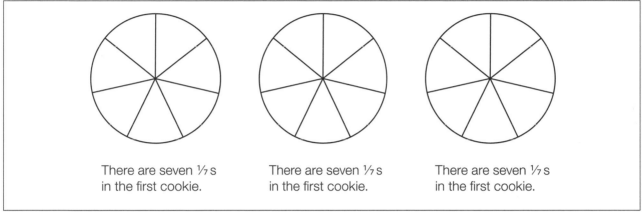

There are seven $\frac{1}{7}$s in the first cookie.　There are seven $\frac{1}{7}$s in the first cookie.　There are seven $\frac{1}{7}$s in the first cookie.

Figure 1.18: A visual model to represent $3 \div \frac{1}{7}$.

So, a prerequisite to creating contexts for $3 \div \frac{1}{7}$ is making sense of dividing whole numbers—specifically, using measurement division as a context to divide whole numbers. This is the case when we divide by a fraction. What about when we divide a fraction by a whole number? Could sharing division be used to represent $\frac{1}{3} \div 2$? What if we had $\frac{1}{3}$ of a cookie and wanted to share it evenly between two friends? Figure 1.19 shows a visual representation of this problem.

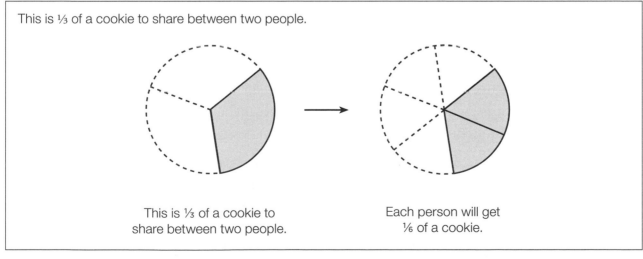

This is $\frac{1}{3}$ of a cookie to share between two people.

This is $\frac{1}{3}$ of a cookie to share between two people.　Each person will get $\frac{1}{6}$ of a cookie.

Figure 1.19: A visual model to represent $\frac{1}{3} \div 2$.

This team conversation—about making sense of the learning standard, connecting it to prerequisites, and linking it with the appropriate mathematical tasks—is important to understanding the types of tasks that provide the desired balance as you design your common formative assessment instruments.

Planning common assessments before the unit begins provides a context for discussing prerequisite knowledge that you may need to address during instruction while making sense of the essential learning standards. It also provides a context for discussing where students might make common errors or hold common misconceptions. Use figure 1.20 to work with your collaborative team to unpack a learning standard for your next common formative assessment instrument.

Directions: Select a learning standard you are planning to address in your next unit assessment, and then respond to the following questions.

1. What prerequisite skills are necessary for this learning standard? How will you assess students' knowledge of these prerequisites?

2. What are common errors related to the learning standard? How will your instruction help to identify and resolve these errors before students take the common unit assessment?

3. How does your conversation around planning common assessment instruments influence your plans for instruction?

Figure 1.20: Preparing common assessment instrument tasks tool.

Visit **go.solution-tree.com/mathematicsatwork** to download a reproducible version of this figure.

Once you identify and explore the prerequisites and common errors, your team is better prepared to develop the common assessment instrument. If this is a new activity for your collaborative team, it might make sense to start with an existing assessment instrument and then adapt it so that it addresses the learning standards comprehensively and provides a balance of cognitive-demand tasks.

Creating an Assessment Instrument

Figure 1.21 highlights a team's first attempt to develop an end-of-unit common assessment instrument. It provides a starting point for the assessment instrument development process for the second-grade content standard cluster *Use place value understanding and properties of operations to add and subtract* (2.NBT). The specific essential learning standards to assess are:

1. Fluently add and subtract within 100 using strategies based on place value, properties of operations, and/or the relationship between addition and subtraction. (2.NBT.5)

2. Add up to four two-digit numbers using strategies based on place value and properties of operations. (2.NBT.6)

3. Add and subtract within 1000, using concrete models or drawings and strategies based on place value, properties of operations, and/or the relationship between addition and subtraction; relate the strategy to a written method. Understand that in adding or subtracting three-digit numbers, one adds or subtracts hundreds and hundreds, tens and tens, ones and ones; and sometimes it is necessary to compose or decompose tens or hundreds. (2.NBT.7) (NGA & CCSSO, 2010, p. 19)

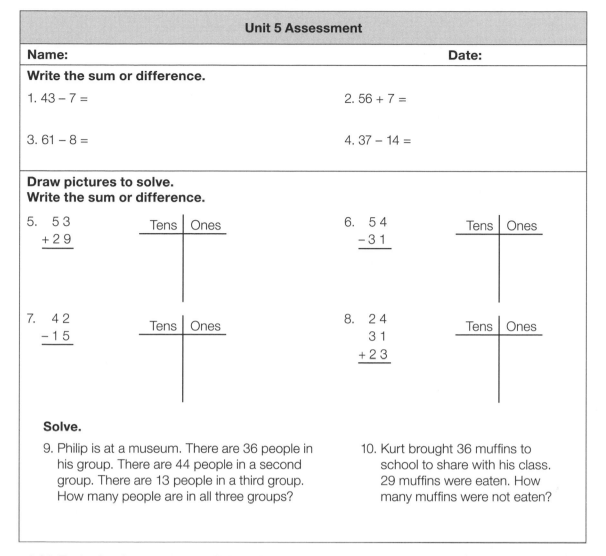

Figure 1.21: End-of-unit test on two-digit addition and subtraction (lower-level cognitive demand only).

Notice that the common assessment is *not* balanced with regard to cognitive demand—one of the requirements of a high-quality assessment instrument. It also lacks some of the other criteria of a high-quality assessment (like the writing of the essential learning standard on the exam), but for now, focus your team's discussion on the balance of cognitive demand of the tasks within the assessment.

As you examine figure 1.21, you will observe that multidigit addition and subtraction are assessed using some problems that require regrouping and some problems that do not. This helps to identify student errors related to regrouping. Notice that problems are presented horizontally as well as vertically. This helps to ensure that students see both formats as representative of addition and subtraction. Also, notice the presence of word problems.

Referencing the essential learning standards, you will see that all sums are within 100 and place value is emphasized, students are required to draw pictures to model composing and decomposing tens, and students add three multidigit numbers. However, since students are not required to explain their thinking, what is not assessed is whether they are using strategies based on place value and properties of operations—an important learning expectation for these standards.

Use figure 1.22 to work with your collaborative team to rewrite some of the items on the end-of-unit assessment instrument from figure 1.21. Use the questions in figure 1.22 as a general guide to create a better balance between higher- and lower-level-cognitive-demand mathematical tasks on your tests.

Directions: With your collaborative team, answer the following questions to check the cognitive-demand balance of your common assessment instruments.

1. What does the current assessment instrument do well?

2. Which tasks on the assessment should remain as lower-level-cognitive-demand mathematical tasks?

3. Which tasks are more easily adapted into higher-level-cognitive-demand mathematical tasks?

Figure 1.22: Checking for cognitive demand balance on the common unit assessment instrument.

Visit **go.solution-tree.com/mathematicsatwork** to download a reproducible version of this figure.

The end-of-unit assessment in figure 1.23 provides an example of an assessment similar to the assessment in figure 1.21 but balanced for cognitive demand. Notice that, for the most part, the numbers are the same. However, students are asked to explain their thinking and to find other ways to solve the problems. When students use procedures, there is an expectation that the procedures will be connected to a demonstration of reasoning.

How does the revised assessment in figure 1.23 compare to the adjustments you made to the assessment with your collaborative team? Your assessment does not need to match; what is important is that the assessment measures student performance on the learning standards, identifies potential misconceptions, and balances cognitive demand.

Spacing. In addition to ensuring your unit assessment instrument meets the balanced cognitive-demand criteria, consider other criteria from the assessment instrument quality-evaluation tool in figure 1.16 (page 35). Notice that the revised version of the assessment is well spaced for student responses and teacher feedback (criterion seven).

Time. You will need to determine the amount of time you want students to spend taking the assessment (criterion seven in figure 1.16). It should be reasonable for the cognitive demands of the assessment and the grade level you teach. While there is no set appropriate amount of time, every team member should agree and commit to following it. It will also be helpful to know and discuss the amount of time grade-level teams above and below you use, if applicable. You may need to adjust your assessment instrument if it is not of appropriate length for your agreed-on test duration.

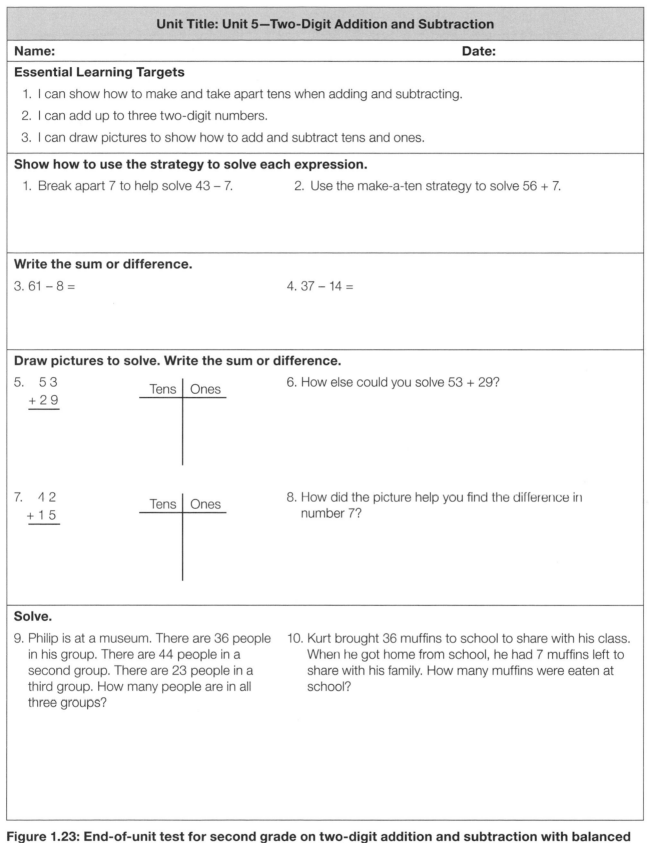

Unit Title: Unit 5—Two-Digit Addition and Subtraction

Name: Date:

Essential Learning Targets

1. I can show how to make and take apart tens when adding and subtracting.

2. I can add up to three two-digit numbers.

3. I can draw pictures to show how to add and subtract tens and ones.

Show how to use the strategy to solve each expression.

1. Break apart 7 to help solve 43 – 7.   2. Use the make-a-ten strategy to solve 56 + 7.

Write the sum or difference.

3. 61 – 8 =   4. 37 – 14 =

Draw pictures to solve. Write the sum or difference.

5. 5 3
   + 2 9   Tens | Ones   6. How else could you solve 53 + 29?

7. 4 2
   + 1 5   Tens | Ones   8. How did the picture help you find the difference in number 7?

Solve.

9. Philip is at a museum. There are 36 people in his group. There are 44 people in a second group. There are 23 people in a third group. How many people are in all three groups?

10. Kurt brought 36 muffins to school to share with his class. When he got home from school, he had 7 muffins left to share with his family. How many muffins were eaten at school?

Figure 1.23: End-of-unit test for second grade on two-digit addition and subtraction with balanced cognitive demand.

In addition to cognitive task balance and time allotment, consider each of the other criteria from figure 1.16 (page 35). For example, identify and emphasize all essential learning standards (criterion one). For young learners, your team might consider it most appropriate to only list the learning standards on the teacher's version of the test. However, for upper-elementary grades, learning standards might take the form of student-friendly "I can . . ." language (see figure 1.23, page 43).

Technology. If you are part of a grades 3–5 team, you will also need to consider the role of technology in your assessments. Since many student state assessments are taken in an online environment, it will be helpful if your students have some experience using technology as a tool in testing.

You should always look for resources that balance conceptual understanding, procedural fluency, and higher- and lower-level cognitive demand. Be sure that all materials you select support the mathematical understanding necessary to achieve the essential learning standards for the unit. For grades 3–5, be sure to allow your students practice in the online format if those are expectations of your state assessments.

As a resource to dig deeper into this issue, consult your state board of education website, NCTM (www.nctm .org), the College Board (www.collegeboard.com/testing), or use the resources for online test samples at Smarter Balanced Assessment Consortium (www.smarterbalanced.org) or PARCC (www.parcconline .org).

Your Team's Progress

As you and your collaborative team focus on developing your common assessment instruments, remember you do not need to design your assessment instruments from scratch. You can use instruments provided with your curriculum materials and adjust them to ensure they address the learning standards, uncover common misconceptions, balance cognitive demand, can be completed in the available time, and use appropriate and clear vocabulary.

It is helpful to diagnose your team's current reality and action prior to launching the unit. Ask each team member to individually assess your team on this third high-leverage team action using the status check tool in table 1.3. Discuss your perception of your team's progress on developing common assessment instruments. It matters less which stage your team is at and more that you and your team members are committed to working together to focus on understanding the learning standards and the best activities and strategies for increasing student understanding and achievement as your team seeks stage IV—sustaining.

Once you have prepared your common unit assessment, your team efforts should turn to creating a scoring rubric for the test and developing proficiency expectations for students. Developing scoring rubrics and proficiency expectations for the common assessment instruments is the fourth high-leverage team action in the before-the-unit planning process. The process of developing scoring rubrics requires your team to reflect and stay focused on the essential learning standards for the unit.

Table 1.3: Before-the-Unit Status Check Tool for HLTA 3—Developing Common Assessment Instruments

Directions: Discuss your perception of your team's progress on the third high-leverage team action—developing common assessment instruments. Defend your reasoning.			
Stage I: Pre-Initiating	**Stage II: Initiating**	**Stage III: Developing**	**Stage IV: Sustaining**
We do not develop or use common assessment instruments.	Some members of our team develop common assessment instruments.	We develop common assessment instruments as a team, but not before the unit begins.	We design and write common assessments as a team before the unit begins.
We do not know if the end-of-unit assessments given by each member of the team are balanced for cognitive demand, provide sufficient time, and use clear language and vocabulary.	We develop end-of-unit common assessments connected to the learning standards, but they are not checked for balance of cognitive demand or clarity.	We develop common end-of-unit assessment instruments connected to the learning standards. They are either balanced for cognitive demand or clear but not both.	We develop common end-of-unit assessments that are clear, balanced, and connected to all aspects of the learning standards for the unit.
We do not know if our assessments are aligned to our instructional practices and reflect the essential learning standards of the unit.	We develop common assessments as a team, but not all members use them to influence their instructional plans for the unit.	Our planning for common assessments influences our instructional plans for the unit.	Our common assessments are deeply aligned with our instructional discussions and practices.

Visit **go.solution-tree.com/mathematicsatwork** to download a reproducible version of this table.

HLTA 4: Developing Scoring Rubrics and Proficiency Expectations for the Common Assessment Instruments

Do you trust me enough to allow me to score and grade your end-of-unit assessments?

—Tim Kanold

Creating a team culture of collaborative scoring and assessment discussions is one of the most important tasks of your grade-level team. It ensures a greater chance for fidelity and accuracy in scoring all assessment instruments, and it eliminates the potential inequity a wide scoring variance from teacher to teacher can cause.

Just as the mathematical tasks and common assessment instruments (tests and quizzes) help you partially answer the second critical question of a PLC—How will we know if they know it?—so do the choices your team makes for scoring the mathematical tasks on the common unit assessments. The benefits of this team action will be discussed further in chapter 3, HLTA 9 and 10 (see page 121).

High-Leverage Team Action	1. What do we want all students to know and be able to do?	2. How will we know if they know it?	3. How will we respond if they don't know it?	4. How will we respond if they do know it?
Before-the-Unit Action				
HLTA 4. Developing scoring rubrics and proficiency expectations for the common assessment instruments		▭		

▭ = Partially addressed with high-leverage team action

The What

Why is this an important before-the-unit high-leverage team activity? HLTA 4 will improve insight into the way you provide instruction pathways for students during the unit. It will also improve the accuracy of your feedback and grading practices at the end of the unit and help create greater team equity in the interpretation of student scores.

By reaching team agreement on the rubric score for each item on the end-of-unit test, you increase the reliability that the feedback for proficiency on the essential learning standards for the unit is accurate, and you increase your ability to ensure students understand the expectations of a solution pathway required to receive full credit on the task.

More important, this action by your team becomes an *inequity eraser* for your students and increases the likelihood that your feedback on their performance will be consistent and accurate across all members of your team.

Determining how to score the assessment instrument involves far more than linking point values to test questions and tasks. As you work on scoring rubrics for tasks in your collaborative team, your instruction during the unit will benefit from:

- Discussing the value of each task relative to the other tasks on the test

- Deciding how you will determine if students have provided a complete solution for full credit relative to the essential learning standard each assessment task (problem) represents

- Deciding what you will do when students' answers are incomplete or incorrect—how their response will be scored

These decisions are typically easier to make and more straightforward with lower-level-cognitive-demand tasks (as may have been the case with your past assessment instruments), but not as clear for the higher-level-cognitive-demand tasks necessary to measure student understanding, reasoning, *and* procedural fluency.

The How

Reconsider the grade K–5 higher-level-cognitive-demand mathematical tasks from figure 1.7 (page 24). Use these tasks to consider what you look for in terms of a complete and correct solution for full credit. Once you have a sense of expectations for student work, you can discuss how to assign point values to the mathematical tasks.

Mathematical Task for Grade K (K.CC.6)
Blake has a number of cubes that is one more than 15. Jessica has a number of cubes that is one less than 17. Who has more cubes? How do you know?

With the kindergarten task, it would be appropriate for students to use manipulatives to make towers of cubes. You would look for students to be able to make a tower that is one more than fifteen and another tower that is one less than seventeen. While it is not required for students to make the towers to solve this problem, it is expected and appropriate according to K.CC.6. You would want students to understand that Blake and Jessica have the same number of cubes and that students are able to verbalize that one more than fifteen is sixteen and one less than seventeen is sixteen, and they are the same.

Mathematical Task for Grade 1 (1.G.3)

Calvin is at a birthday party where children will be sitting at tables. The chairs are already set up at each table. At one table, there are two chairs, and the mini birthday cake is cut in halves. At another table, there are four chairs, and a mini birthday cake of the same size is cut in fourths.

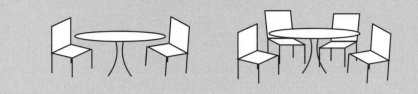

Calvin thinks he will get the same amount of cake wherever he sits because he will get a piece of birthday cake no matter what. Tell if you agree or disagree, and say why.

First-grade students will need to make sense of what it means for the same-size whole to be cut into halves and fourths. They need to see that the goal of this problem is to compare the size of the piece of birthday cake Calvin will receive. Finally, they need to disagree with Calvin and be able to indicate that the same-size cake cut into fourths will lead to smaller pieces than if it is cut into halves.

Mathematical Task for Grade 2 (2.NBT.5)

Alex was partway finished with a problem in mathematics class in which she needed to find 48 + 25 when it was time to leave for lunch. The teacher picked up Alex's paper and was not sure if Alex was correct. Describe how Alex could be correct as well as the last step she still had to complete.

$$48 + 25$$
$$40 + 20 = 60$$
$$8 + 2 = 10$$
$$60 + 10 = 70$$

This second-grade task can be challenging for students and teachers. Students will likely see that 48 can be broken apart into 40 + 8, and 25 can be described as 20 + 5, so the first step of finding 40 + 20 should be fine. However, the second step often causes some confusion. Alex broke the 5 into 2 + 3 so that she could combine the 8 from 48 with the 2 from 5 to make a 10. She then added 60 + 10 to get 70. She still has to add the 3 from the 5 to the 70 to get 73. A correct answer from the student would involve explaining where the 2 came from as well as adding 3 to the 70 to complete the problem.

Mathematical Task for Grade 3 (3.OA.4)

A student in your class is asked to solve 6 × 7 without drawing pictures. The student does not know the fact. Provide two different ways the student could use multiplication to solve the fact by using other facts the student might know.

This third-grade task is one in which students may demonstrate understanding of the solution to 6 × 7 but not follow the requirements of the task. For example, students might draw pictures as groups of objects and arrays to solve the problem in two different ways, but they would not be using other multiplication facts to find the product. Your team will need to determine if this sort of answer would receive full credit. There are many appropriate ways to assign credit; your team just needs to agree. Ultimately, your goal must be for students to use fact strategies like doubling 3 × 7, tripling 2 × 7, and breaking apart one of the factors to provide two different paths to the solution, and your plans for instruction should reflect this.

Mathematical Task for Grade 4 (4.OA.2)

Write four different story problems to correspond to the following expression: 46 ÷ 4. Each problem should lead to a different answer. The answers to the problems should be 11½, 12, 11, and 2. Do not use the words *estimate, about,* or *round* in your problems.

This task requires fourth-grade students to first find the quotient of 46 divided by 4 and then come up with contexts that would cause the remainder to be interpreted in different ways. For a quotient of 11½, the context needs to include something that can be cut in half, like a cookie. For a quotient of 12, the context must be something that cannot be cut in half, like a rollercoaster car. With a quotient of 11, the context needs to describe a situation in which not all forty-six items will be used, like sharing forty-six books equally among four groups. The 2 as an answer describes the remainder itself—it could be the two books that were left over within the previous context. This higher-level-cognitive-demand mathematical task requires that a student, or group of students, makes sense of all of those types of contexts to completely and correctly answer the question.

Mathematical Task for Grade 5 (5.NF.4a and 5.NF.6)

Write a word problem for ⅔ × ¾, and then use a visual model to solve it that is supportive of the context used in your word problem.

In grade 5, students are to create story problems and use visual models to solve fraction multiplication problems. In this task, you can describe ⅔ × ¾ as finding an area or finding a part of a part of an object or group; we can think of this as finding ⅔ of a group of ¾ of a whole. An example of each along with a visual model to represent it appears in figure 1.24 (page 50).

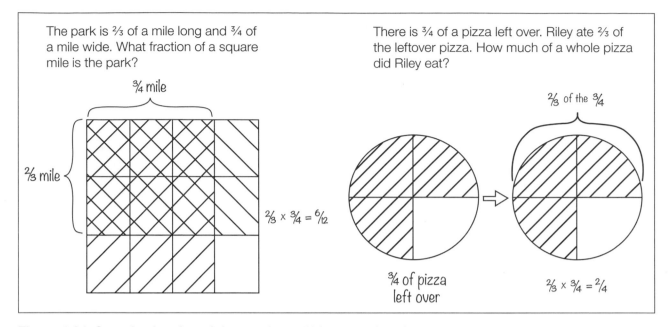

The park is ⅔ of a mile long and ¾ of a mile wide. What fraction of a square mile is the park?

¾ mile

⅔ mile

⅔ × ¾ = ⁶⁄₁₂

There is ¾ of a pizza left over. Riley ate ⅔ of the leftover pizza. How much of a whole pizza did Riley eat?

⅔ of the ¾

¾ of pizza left over

⅔ × ¾ = ²⁄₄

Figure 1.24: Sample visual models to solve a fifth-grade fraction multiplication problem.

Notice that the visual representation depends on the context of the problem. Students need to make sense of both the word problem and the visual model to correctly and fully respond to this task, and teachers need to check carefully that the visual model matches the context (see Dixon & Tobias, 2013, for an in-depth discussion of related tasks). Therefore, it is likely that points would be assigned to each part.

In developing the scoring rubric, the actual points for scoring are less important than the team conversation that occurs as you determine *how* to assign the points. This must be a joint decision for your team to function well.

Use the collaborative team task scoring discussion tool in figure 1.25 to work with your collaborative team to examine the K–5 task appropriate to your grade level. Discuss point values you would use when assigning a score to the task if it was on an end-of-unit assessment.

Discussions about proficiency scores for each end-of-unit assessment task provide a means for unpacking the items to determine how to score them in specific ways. It is important that, if possible, this team activity occurs *before the unit begins* as your discussions around this activity will likely influence your eventual instruction.

Consider mathematical task number five on the assessment instrument from figure 1.23 (page 43). How would you assign a score to it? Would you give a point for drawing tens and ones appropriately? Would you assign a point for a loop that groups ten ones to show one ten? Would you assign one point for the correct answer or would that be worth more than one point relative to the others? The actual point values matter less than coming to consensus in your collaborative team regarding how you will assign points.

Directions: With your collaborative team, discuss scoring for the K–5 task appropriate to your grade level from figure 1.6 (page 35). Respond to each of the following questions.

1. What would you require students to demonstrate in order to receive full credit for the task?

2. How would you assign a score for proficiency to each part of the response?

3. How would you and your collaborative team reach consensus on the relative worth of the tasks?

Figure 1.25: Collaborative team task scoring discussion tool.

Visit **go.solution-tree.com/mathematicsatwork** to download a reproducible version of this figure.

Work in your team to assign points to the revised end-of-unit assessment instrument in figure 1.23 (page 43). Use the prompts from figure 1.26, and answer the questions provided for each task on the assessment.

Directions: Within your collaborative team, answer each of the following questions in relation to each item on the assessment.

1. Which specific learning standard does each task address? Align the tasks with the appropriate "I can . . ." statement.

2. What work do you expect students to demonstrate in order to successfully respond to each mathematical task and receive full credit?

3. Which tasks provide students with the best opportunities to demonstrate specific Mathematical Practices, and what are those practices?

4. How do the scores assigned reflect your priorities for proficiency on each essential learning standard of the unit?

Figure 1.26: Assessment instrument alignment and scoring rubric tool.

Visit **go.solution-tree.com/mathematicsatwork** to download a reproducible version of this figure.

Creating a Scoring Rubric

There are many appropriate ways to construct a scoring rubric for a given assessment, and scoring rubrics rarely take into account *every* solution pathway. Your scoring rubric should assign points based on the use of strategies but not limit the ways that students may demonstrate their understanding. What follows is just one example of a scoring rubric for the end-of-unit test highlighted in figure 1.23 (page 43). You and your collaborative team should compare your scoring rubric to the sample end-of-unit test-scoring rubric in figure 1.27. Discuss how they are similar and different and what aspects you prefer from each. Notice how Mathematical Practice 7—"Look for and make use of structure"—is evident in the scoring rubric with respect to the use of the make-a-ten strategy to solve problems. By focusing on the Mathematical Practices when planning common formative assessments, you and your team will be more likely to emphasize them during instruction.

The two-digit addition and subtraction end-of-unit test from figure 1.23 assesses three essential learning standards for student proficiency.

1. I can show how to make and take apart tens when adding and subtracting (assessment tasks one and two).

2. I can add up to three two-digit numbers (assessment tasks three, four, nine, and ten).

3. I can draw pictures to show how to add and subtract tens and ones (assessment tasks five, six, seven, and eight).

Depending on the cognitive demand of the tasks, and the levels of complex reasoning the task requires, the value of each task is differentiated for scoring purposes. For example, tasks one and two were worth three points each, and tasks three and four were worth two points each. Tasks one and two required several steps in the answer and specific strategies from the students. Tasks three and four required only that the students determine the difference. Students might only have the option of earning a score of 0, 1, or 2 for each of tasks three and four, or they might be given partial proficiency depending on their error. This would be a topic for discussion in your collaborative team. While the balance of your rubric scores for your team may differ from those we suggest here, you should come to a consensus within your team.

Your team should set proficiency expectations for each of the three essential learning standards for the assessment. In figure 1.27, the total score possible for each essential standard on the end-of-unit assessment is:

1. I can show how to make and take apart tens when adding and subtracting (assessment tasks one and two for a score of 6).

2. I can add up to three two-digit numbers (assessment tasks three, four, nine, and ten for a score of 8).

3. I can draw pictures to show how to add and subtract tens and ones (assessment tasks five, six, seven, and eight for a score of 11).

Two-Digit Addition and Subtraction End-of-Unit Test-Scoring Rubric					
Total Score: 25					
	Scoring Rubric	**Points**		**Scoring Rubric**	**Points**
1.	Break apart 7 into 3 and 4.	1	2.	Break apart 7 into 4 and 3.	1
	Subtract 3 from 43.	1		Add 56 and 4 to get 60.	1
	Subtract 4 from 40.	1		Add 60 and 3 to get 63.	1
	(Process supports Mathematical Practice 7.)			(Process supports Mathematical Practice 7.)	
3.	Subtract correctly to get 53.	2	4.	Subtract correctly to get 23.	2
5.	Represent 53 as 5 tens 3 ones.	1	6.	Represent solution to 53 + 29 correctly.	1
	Represent 29 as 2 tens 9 ones.	1		Use a strategy different from the one in number 5.	1
	Combine ones as 1 ten 2 ones.	1			
	Add to get 82.	1			
	(Drawing supports Mathematical Practice 7.)				
7.	Represent 42 as 4 tens 2 ones.	1	8.	Describe a process for finding the difference.	1
	Show in drawing that 15 is subtracted from 42.*	1		Process matches the picture.	1
	Subtract correctly to get 27.	1		(Reasoning supports Mathematical Practice 7.)	
	(Drawing supports Mathematical Practice 7.)				
9.	Determine the operation is addition.	1	10.	Determine the operation is subtraction.	1
	Add correctly to get 103.	1		Subtract correctly to get 29.	1

* Notice there is not a requirement to draw 1 ten and 5 ones for 15. This is because students might correctly draw both 42 and 15 to solve the problem or just draw 42 and cross out 15 from the 42 that are drawn.

Figure 1.27: Sample end-of-unit test-scoring rubric for figure 1.23 (page 43).

Visit **go.solution-tree.com/mathematicsatwork** to download a reproducible version of this figure.

Your team should decide on the level necessary for student proficiency on the learning standards for the end-of-unit assessment's three essential standards. Your team's response to students who do or do not achieve the learning proficiency target is further discussed in chapter 3 and HLTA 9 (see page 123).

You can work with your collaborative team and use the prompts about the scoring of your assessments as stated in figure 1.28 (page 54), the Assessment Instrument Alignment and Scoring Rubric Tool.

Directions: Work with the end-of-unit assessment and answer each of the following standard alignment and scoring rubric questions.

1. Which essential learning standard does each task address, and how do you know?

2. What do you expect students to demonstrate in order to successfully respond to and receive full credit for each task on the assessment?

3. How will you assign partial credit?

4. To which Mathematical Practices does each task connect (or not)?

5. What is the scoring value or point value assigned to each task, and how many total points should be used for this end-of-unit assessment?

6. Are there any questions on the test you would want to ask differently? If so, how would that impact the point value you would assign to the test question or task?

7. How many points correct would a student need for each essential learning standard in order to be considered proficient for that standard (proficiency targets)?

Figure 1.28: Assessment instrument alignment and scoring rubric tool.

Visit **go.solution-tree.com/mathematicsatwork** to download a reproducible version of this figure.

It is not so much that there is one right answer to the issue of the scoring points used for your end-of-unit assessments. What is important is that your team uses the same scoring scale, that your team bases the scoring rubric on a decided standard (such as the complexity of reasoning required by the assessment task, or a proficiency scale based on lower- or higher-level cognitive demand), and that each member of your team honors the scoring rubric agreement chosen. This equity pursuit will allow for your scoring of student work to be held to a higher standard of accuracy, and is discussed in more detail with HLTA 9 in chapter 3 (see page 123).

Setting Proficiency Targets

Notice the last question in figure 1.28: How many points correct would a student need for each essential learning standard in order to be considered proficient for that standard (proficiency targets)?

Your grade-level team should decide what level of student performance will be required to be considered proficient in each of the essential learning standards for the end-of-unit assessment. Your team should know the learning score target you will expect each student to obtain for each learning standard to be considered proficient for that essential learning standard. Your team's response to students who do or do not achieve the learning proficiency target is the action described in HLTA 9 and discussed further in chapter 3.

There is a type of standards-based grading practice gaining popularity in grades K–8 across the United States. It involves measuring students' proficiency on well-defined course learning standards (Marzano, 2009). Although many districts adopt standards-based grading *in addition* to traditional grades, standards-based grading can replace traditional point-based grades. If this is the case at your school, and you want more information on standards-based grading, you can go to marzanoresearch.com to review Robert Marzano's (2009) *Formative Assessment and Standards-Based Grading* or *A School Leader's Guide to Standards-Based Grading* (Heflebower, Hoegh, & Warrick, 2014) and learn more about the use of proficiency scales to score student work and measure student progress.

Your Team's Progress

It is helpful to diagnose your team's current reality and action prior to launching the unit. Ask each team member to individually assess your team on the fourth high-leverage team action using the status check tool in table 1.4 (page 56). Discuss your perception of your team's progress on developing scoring rubrics and proficiency expectations for the common assessment instruments. It matters less which stage your team is at and more that you and your team members are committed to working together and understanding the various student pathways for demonstrating solutions to the mathematical tasks on your common assessments as your team seeks stage IV—sustaining.

These first four high-leverage team actions give you and your team:

- A direct focus on your unit-by-unit decisions regarding the essential learning standards
- Insight into mathematical tasks and activities that support your work during the unit
- Understanding of common assessments you can use to determine whether or not students have attained knowledge of the essential learning standards
- Guidelines for how to score student work and set proficiency expectations for each essential learning standard of the unit

There is one major high-leverage, equity-based team action left to complete before you launch into the unit and your instruction: planning for and using common homework assignments.

Table 1.4: Before-the-Unit Status Check Tool for HTLA 4—Developing Scoring Rubrics and Proficiency Expectations for the Common Assessment Instruments

Directions: Discuss your perception of your team's progress on the fourth high-leverage team action—developing scoring rubrics and proficiency expectations for the common assessment instruments. Defend your reasoning.

Stage I: Pre-Initiating	Stage II: Initiating	Stage III: Developing	Stage IV: Sustaining
We do not use common scoring rubrics on our assessments.	We discuss our scoring and grading practices collaboratively.	We create scoring rubrics for our common unit assessments collaboratively.	We create dependable scoring rubrics for all tasks on the common unit assessments as a collaborative team.
Each teacher establishes his or her own scoring system for their independent assessments.	We have not yet reached agreement on how to score the tasks on our common assessments.	We discuss and reach agreement on a student's complete response to receive full credit on each task for our common assessments.	We design assessment rubrics to align with students' reasoning about the mathematics in each essential learning standard for the unit.
We do not know the scoring and grading practices other members of our team use.	We use scoring rubrics independently, and do not discuss our use of scoring rubrics with other members of the team.	We use the common end-of-unit assessment scoring rubrics for measuring student proficiency on each learning standard but don't discuss them as a team.	We use the common end-of-unit assessment scoring rubrics for measuring student proficiency on each learning standard and discuss them as a team.
We do not set student proficiency targets for each essential learning standard of the unit.	We set student proficiency targets independently, but do not know the proficiency targets other members of our team use for each essential learning standard of the unit.	We collaboratively set student proficiency target performances on the end-of-unit assessment for some, but not all, of the essential learning standards of the unit.	We collaboratively set student proficiency target performances on the end-of-unit assessment for each essential learning standard of the unit.

Visit **go.solution-tree.com/mathematicsatwork** to download a reproducible version of this table.

HLTA 5: Planning and Using Common Homework Assignments

Assign work that is worthy of their best effort (problem solving and reasoning).

—Linda Darling-Hammond

By using homework for practice in self-assessment and complex thinking skills, we can put students in charge of the learning process.

—Cathy Vatterott

Planning common homework assignments is another way your team reaches agreement on the second critical question of a PLC, How will we know if they know it?

High-Leverage Team Action	1. What do we want all students to know and be able to do?	2. How will we know if they know it?	3. How will we respond if they don't know it?	4. How will we respond if they do know it?
Before-the-Unit Action				
HLTA 5. Planning and using common homework assignments	▨▢	▨		

▨ = Fully addressed with high-leverage team action

▨▢ = Partially addressed with high-leverage team action

The mathematical tasks and problems you assign as homework should help you and your students accurately answer the question, How will we know if we are understanding the daily learning objectives from the lesson? Thus, your team needs to reach agreement on the purpose, coherence, rigor, and length of homework assignments. In addition, your team needs to agree on how the homework will be used and communicate this to students, parents, and support staff. Why is this an important before-the-unit high-leverage team action? Once again, your team's work to develop common homework assignments for the unit before it begins becomes a potential inequity eraser for you and your students. Also, mathematics homework in elementary school is often an area that lacks clarity and purpose for students, parents, intervention support personnel, and most importantly, you. Your team asks, "Why do we give students homework? What is the purpose of homework? Why won't students do their homework? How is homework assigned for a grade?" The very idea of mathematics homework in elementary school, and what to do with it, is often a conundrum.

Is homework really an essential element to the process of student learning? The short answer is yes, but the best protocols to follow for homework are not quite as clear. What is clear is that:

1. The assignment of independent practice or homework cannot be a superficial exercise for you or your team.

2. Anyone who is an expert at anything devotes significant time to practice (Gladwell, 2008).

3. If we deny students an opportunity for independent practice, we deny them the very thing they need to develop real competence (Anderson, Reder, & Simon, 1995).

The homework you assign, as well as the way you think about homework as a class activity—the way you use it as a formative task to guide instruction—needs to be a carefully thought out and planned for team discussion, agreement, and activity *before* the unit begins.

The What

You should provide an outline of the team-developed homework assignments to your students, parents, and support staff in advance of teaching the unit with the understanding that your team will modify the assignments during the unit as necessary to address specific student learning needs.

Common Core–type learning standards expect students to learn mathematics in ways that often do not match how their parents learned mathematics—and maybe even how you learned. Because of this, homework often leaves parents at a loss with how to help their children. In many instances, parents' only way of supporting their children is to tell them to solve the problems the way they learned to solve the problems. This often results in parents teaching procedures prior to the teacher's instruction of the learning standards.

It can also result in frustration on the part of parents and their children. Once you and your collaborative team reach consensus on homework protocols—the policies and goals for homework, along with the essential learning standards the homework supports—you must make them clear to parents (such as through newsletters and school meetings or email). You will need to make an ongoing commitment to communication.

Despite the dilemma with parents and homework, research does indicate that homework can be helpful in improving student achievement (Cooper, 2008b). Marzano (2007) finds that to have a positive effect, homework should have a clear purpose communicated to students. The purpose may be to deepen students' conceptual understanding, enhance procedural fluencies, and allow students an opportunity for formative practice around higher-level-cognitive-demand mathematical tasks.

Research also supports the idea of *spaced* (sometimes called *distributed* or *spiral*) versus *massed* homework practice during the unit of study (Hattie, 2012; Rohrer & Pashler, 2007) as having a significant impact on student learning. That is, provide homework assignment (practice) tasks that are spaced throughout the unit, allowing your students to cycle back and perform distributed practice on prior learning standards, including those learned earlier in the unit, in previous units, or possibly in the previous grade level.

As each teacher on your team begins to honor high-leverage team actions 1 to 4 (teaching to the same set of essential learning standards and designing high-quality common assessments) for your course, then it is a natural outcome that the nature of practice for student learning *outside of class* (homework) would be designed from the same core set of problems for each student, no matter the teacher for the course.

The How

Understanding the purpose of mathematics homework on a daily basis during each unit is your first step to significantly improving current homework practice.

Understanding the Purpose of Homework

Use the questions in figure 1.29 (page 60), the Collaborative Homework Assignment Protocol Discussion Tool, to help you and your team develop a better understanding of the purpose, content, and expected protocols for the unit's homework assignments. You can also use these prompts for team discussion with vertical K–3 and 3–5 teams as you examine mathematics homework protocols and progressions across all grade levels in your building.

Your answers to the questions in figure 1.29 will likely vary a bit for each of your collaborative teams, but they should be consistent with the expectations of your grade-level program, school, or district. The expectation is that your collaborative team will reach full agreement on your responses to the questions in figure 1.29 as you work together (before the unit begins) to select appropriate independent practice tasks (homework problems) for students to do outside of the classroom.

Your responses as individuals and as a team to these questions will reveal some of your current beliefs about assigning mathematics homework. In response to question 1 in figure 1.29, Why do we assign homework for each unit's lessons? What is the purpose of homework? It is important to note that the primary purpose of homework is *not* summative. Homework should not be assigned to students in order to assign a grade. In fact, homework should generally not count for more than 5 to 10 percent of the total student grade. Because homework is a formative learning activity—an opportunity for students to practice and obtain feedback and improve learning outside of class time—it should not constitute so much of a student's grade that it is not reflective of actual in-class performance.

The primary purpose of mathematics homework for elementary school students is *independent practice*. More importantly, *successful* independent practice. That is, students must understand and use homework as an opportunity for a self-guided formative assessment learning process, while you are not in the room (Hattie, 2012). Independent practice can be with other students, with other adults, or with help from YouTube or other social media resources as appropriate. However, your students, while outside of class and away from you as their teacher and your guided practice, must practice mathematics problems and connect those tasks to the essential learning standards.

Students need to complete homework because of the importance of formative assessment and successful practice as a critical part of their long-term learning process. In class, students do need teacher modeling and lots of peer-to-peer guided practice (HLTA 7 in chapter 2 of this handbook); then, outside of class and in a timely fashion, they need to do accurate independent practice with feedback (self-feedback or with peers) and then take action, well before they are back in your class the next day.

The work of your collaborative team is to decide, before the unit begins, what and how much homework to provide for additional student independent practice. Your team must decide how you will communicate the homework assignments to students and parents. Ultimately, the work of your collaborative team is to decide the role homework plays as part of your classroom protocols.

Directions: Use the following prompts to guide discussion of the unit's homework assignments.

Purpose of homework:

1. Why do we assign homework for each unit's lessons? What is the purpose of homework?

Nature of homework:

2. What is the proper number of mathematical tasks for daily homework assigned during the unit? In other words, how much time should students spend on homework?

3. What is the proper rigor (cognitive-demand expectations) of the mathematical tasks for homework assigned during the unit?

4. What is the proper distribution of tasks for homework to ensure spaced practice (cyclical review) for our students?

5. How do our daily homework assignments align to the learning standard expectations for the unit?

6. How will we reach consensus on unit homework assignments in order to ensure coherence to the student learning and practice expectations?

Use of homework:

7. How should we grade or score homework assignments?

8. What will we do if students do not complete their homework assignments?

9. How will we go over the homework in class?

10. How will we communicate the common unit homework assignments to students, parents, and support staff?

Figure 1.29: Collaborative homework assignment protocol discussion tool.

Visit **go.solution-tree.com/mathematicsatwork** to download a reproducible version of this figure.

Using Effective Homework Protocols

From a rigor and coherence point of view, the homework you assign for a unit of study must be the same for all students in each grade level in your building. Give team-developed homework assignments to your students and parents in advance of teaching the unit with the understanding that your team can and will modify the assignments during the unit as necessary to address specific student learning needs. To check how your team is currently doing with respect to homework, you can use figure 1.30 (page 62) to measure the quality of your current homework assignments and your progress with respect to high-quality mathematics homework procedures.

You and your team can use figure 1.31 (page 63) as a model. This homework assignment sheet provides the prerequisite learning standards and the essential learning standards for the unit in student-friendly language. Parents are able to see how the work to be completed at home is distributed throughout the unit and also how the homework connects to daily learning objectives.

Homework that provides a review of previous work and helps prepare for work to come has been linked to improved student achievement (Cooper, 2008a). As you develop your team's homework protocol, consider the following.

- **Homework purpose:** The primary purpose of homework should be to allow the student the opportunity for *independent practice* on learning standards mastered in class during guided practice and small-group discourse. Homework can also provide a chance for the student to practice mathematical tasks that relate to previous learning standards or tasks that reflect prerequisite learning standards for the next unit.

- **Homework length:** How much time should daily homework take students to complete? How many problems should it entail? Homework should not be lengthy (Cooper, 2008b), so teachers should take care about what they assign. Take into account the cognitive demand of the tasks or problems you assign. Homework tasks as a general rule should not take more than thirty minutes of time outside of class at the upper elementary grades and much less time in the earlier grades.

- **Homework task selection:** The homework your school curriculum or textbook includes is not necessarily appropriate for your students without some adjustments with which your team agrees. Make sure that all tasks are necessary as part of independent practice, have spaced practice and not massed practice, and align to the stated or prerequisite learning standards of the unit. As Doug Rohrer and Harold Pashler (2010) note, "If a given amount of study time is distributed or *spaced* across multiple sessions rather than massed into a single session, performance on a delayed final test is improved—a finding known as the *spacing* effect" (p. 407).

- **Homework focus in class:** Once your collaborative team determines homework, focus on how to address homework in class, the type of feedback that teachers will give to students, and what will occur if students do not complete the homework. If you spend most of the class time going over homework, your team must revisit the amount and content of what you assign. It could be that your team assigned too much homework or that students did not achieve an appropriate level of mastery prior to practice of the learning standard.

High-Quality Homework Indicators	Description of Level 1	Requirements of the Indicator Are Not Present	Limited Requirements of This Indicator Are Present	Substantially Meets the Requirements of the Indicator	Fully Achieves the Requirements of the Indicator	Description of Level 4
The primary purpose of homework is independent practice.	Homework is primarily assigned to give a student a grade. Homework counts more than 10 percent of a student's total grade.	1	2	3	4	Homework is understood as primarily for independent practice and a formative assessment learning loop for students. Homework counts no more than 10 percent of a student's grade.
Homework assignments are the same for every teacher on the course team.	Each teacher on the team creates his or her own homework assignments and does not share with others.	1	2	3	4	Common homework assignments are developed collaboratively by the team and are the same for all students in the grade level or course.
All homework assignments for the unit are given to the students before the unit begins.	Students find out homework assignments each day or each week as the unit progresses.	1	2	3	4	Students are provided all unit homework assignments—electronically or with a handout—as the unit begins.
Homework assignments for the unit are appropriately balanced for cognitive demand.	Homework practice problems are not balanced for rigor. Emphasis is on lower-cognitive-demand tasks.	1	2	3	4	Homework practice is appropriately balanced with higher- and lower-cognitive-demand tasks.
All practice problem answers are given to the students in advance of the homework assignments.	Students must wait until the next day to receive answers or solutions to homework practice problems.	1	2	3	4	Students are able to check their solutions during independent practice and are expected to rework the problems if not correct the first time.
Homework assignments for each unit exhibit spaced and mass practice.	The homework assignments represent superficial thought as to the problems chosen and consist of massed practice.	1	2	3	4	The homework assignments represent carefully chosen problems or tasks. Spaced practice from several lessons of the unit or previous units is included in addition to massed practice.
Daily homework is aligned to the essential learning standards of the unit.	Students are not able to make connections between the daily homework practice problems and the learning standards of the unit.	1	2	3	4	Students connect the homework practice as essential to helping them demonstrate knowledge of the essential learning standards of the unit.
Limited time is spent going over homework in class.	Students and teacher spend fifteen to twenty-five minutes (or more) in class going over the homework answers and solutions. The teacher does most of the work as the students watch.	1	2	3	4	At most, five to seven minutes of class time is used discussing the homework. It is primarily a peer-to-peer class activity facilitated by the teacher.

Figure 1.30: Homework quality diagnostic tool.

Visit **go.solution-tree.com/mathematicsatwork** to download a reproducible version of this figure.

Homework Assignment Sheet	
Unit 4: Multiplication Facts and Strategies	

What I've already learned:

- I can already show multiplication as groups of objects.
- I can already use objects to multiply.
- I can already use repeated addition to multiply.

Essential learning standards:

- I can use the doubling strategy to multiply.
- I can change the order of factors to use a fact I know.
- I can use the break-apart strategy to multiply.
- I can represent multiplication strategies with equations.

Learning Objectives	Homework*
Multiply with 2.	Practice book page 65, numbers 4, 5, 7, and 18; practice book page 66, numbers 5 and 6
Multiply with 4.	Practice book page 67, numbers 2, 3, 10, and 11; practice book page 68, numbers 1 and 2
Use doubles to multiply.	Describe how you can use 4×6 to find the product of 8×6.
Multiply with 8.	Practice multiplication facts for 2s, 4s, and 8s.
Model with arrays.	Draw arrays to show 4×3, 3×4, 5×3, and 3×5.
Algebra: Use the commutative property.	Practice book page 73, numbers 1–8; practice book page 74, numbers 1 and 2
Multiply with 5.	Practice book page 77, numbers 5–14; practice book page 78, numbers 1 and 2
Break apart numbers to multiply.	A student in your class is asked to solve 6×7 without drawing pictures. The student does not know the fact. Provide two different ways the student could use multiplication to solve the fact by using other facts the student might know.
Multiply with 3 and 6.	Practice book page 85, numbers 3–13 odd; practice book page 87, numbers 5–10
Multiply with 7 and 9.	Practice book page 89, numbers 7–9; practice book page 90, number 1; practice book page 93, numbers 2–4
Algebra: Use the associative and distributive properties.	Practice book page 99, numbers 1–8; practice book page 100, number 2; practice book page 101, numbers 5–12

Specific assignment dates will be provided as the unit progresses.

Figure 1.31: Sample unit homework assignment sheet for grade 3.

Visit **go.solution-tree.com/mathematicsatwork** to download a reproducible version of this figure.

Special note: Since the main purpose of homework is independent practice, limit the amount of time given in class to grade, score, or go over homework to no more than five to seven minutes a day. Otherwise, your students will learn to wait to do homework until you show them in class the next day, which defeats the purpose of independent and timely practice. These processes and procedures should be consistent from teacher to teacher within your collaborative team.

Your Team's Progress

It is helpful to diagnose your team's current reality and action prior to launching the unit. Ask each team member to individually assess your team on the fifth high-leverage team action using the status check tool in table 1.5. Discuss perceptions of your team's progress on planning and using common homework assignments. It matters less which stage your team is at and more that you and your team members are committed to collaboratively defining the purpose of homework, using the same common homework assignments and protocols, and communicating those assignments to students, parents, and colleagues as your team seeks stage IV—sustaining.

Table 1.5: Before-the-Unit Status Check Tool for HLTA 5—Planning and Using Common Homework Assignments

Directions: Discuss your perception of your team's progress on the fifth high-leverage team action—planning and using common homework assignments. Defend your reasoning.			
Stage I: Pre-Initiating	**Stage II: Initiating**	**Stage III: Developing**	**Stage IV: Sustaining**
We do not have a clear purpose for why we assign homework.	We have *established* a clear purpose for homework, but it is not independent and formative student practice.	We have *developed* the shared purpose of using homework as independent formative student practice.	We have *implemented* the shared purpose of homework as independent formative student practice.
We do not plan or use common homework assignments and do not know the homework assignments given by other members of our team.	We discuss homework assignments and have not yet reached collaborative agreement on the nature of those assignments for each unit.	We collaboratively *plan* and develop common homework assignments for each unit.	We collaboratively *use* common homework assignments for each unit.
We do not know the nature of the homework protocols used for the assignments given by other members of our team.	We discuss the nature of the homework protocols used for the assignments given by other members of our team, but do not agree on those protocols.	We have team agreement on developed homework protocols including limited number of tasks, spaced practice, balance of cognitive demand, and alignment to the essential learning standards.	We have complete team agreement on homework protocols including limited number of tasks, spaced practice, balance of cognitive demand, and alignment to the essential learning standards. And we use those protocols with our students.
We do not know how other members of our team go over homework in class.	We discuss how we go over homework in class but do not agree on what we should do.	We discuss how we *go over* homework in class and agree on what we should do with homework during class.	We discuss how we *go over* homework in class, agree on what we should do, and implement that agreement.
We do not know how other members of our team count homework as a percent of the student's total grade.	We know how others count homework for a grade, but we each do it our own way.	We grade homework the same each day, but we count it differently from other team members as a percent of the total student grade.	We have complete team agreement on how homework should be used and accounted for as part of the students' total grade.

Visit **go.solution-tree.com/mathematicsatwork** to download a reproducible version of this table.

As your team seeks the sustaining stage, you will increase the rigor, coherence, and fidelity of the independent practice (homework) all students are expected to do during the unit for your grade level.

Setting Your Before-the-Unit Priorities for Team Action

When your school functions within a PLC culture, your grade-level collaborative team makes a commitment to reach agreement on the five before-the-unit-begins high-leverage team actions outlined in this chapter.

1. Making sense of the agreed-on essential learning standards (content and practices) and pacing

2. Identifying higher-level-cognitive-demand mathematical tasks

3. Developing common assessment instruments

4. Developing scoring rubrics and proficiency expectations for the common assessment instruments

5. Planning and using common homework assignments

As a team, reflect on the stage with which you identified for each of these five team actions. Based on the results, what should be your team's priority? Use figure 1.32 (page 66) to focus your time and energy on actions that are most urgent in your team's preparation for the next unit. You and your team cannot focus on everything. Focus on fewer things, and make those things matter at a deep level of implementation.

The five high-leverage team actions in this chapter combine to form step one of the teaching-assessing-learning cycle (see figure 1.1, page 8) and will help you prepare for the rigors and challenges of teaching and learning during the unit. They are also linked to teacher actions that will significantly impact student learning in your class.

In chapter 2, we turn our attention to steps two and three of the teaching-assessing-learning cycle, which focus on implementing formative assessment classroom strategies and students taking action on in-class formative assessment feedback. We also focus on supporting student engagement in the Mathematical Practices to promote deeper understanding of mathematical content through the use of higher-level-cognitive-demand mathematical tasks. The Mathematical Practices lesson-planning tool described in chapter 2 provides one avenue for organizing your collaborative team's work.

Directions: Identify (circle) the stage you rated your team for each of the five high-leverage team actions, and provide a brief rationale. When you are ready, discuss your ratings as a team.

1. Making sense of the agreed-on essential learning standards (content and practices) and pacing

   Stage I: Pre-Initiating   Stage II: Initiating   Stage III: Developing   Stage IV: Sustaining

   Reason: _____

   _____

   _____

2. Identifying higher-level-cognitive-demand mathematical tasks

   Stage I: Pre-Initiating   Stage II: Initiating   Stage III: Developing   Stage IV: Sustaining

   Reason: _____

   _____

   _____

3. Developing common assessment instruments

   Stage I: Pre-Initiating   Stage II: Initiating   Stage III: Developing   Stage IV: Sustaining

   Reason: _____

   _____

   _____

4. Developing scoring rubrics and proficiency expectations for the common assessment instruments

   Stage I: Pre-Initiating   Stage II: Initiating   Stage III: Developing   Stage IV: Sustaining

   Reason: _____

   _____

   _____

5. Planning and using common homework assignments

   Stage I: Pre-Initiating   Stage II: Initiating   Stage III: Developing   Stage IV: Sustaining

   Reason: _____

   _____

   _____

With your collaborative team, respond to the red light, yellow light, and green light prompts for the high-leverage team actions that you and your team believe are most urgent.

Red light: Indicate one activity you will stop doing that limits effective implementation of each high-leverage team action.

Yellow light: Indicate one activity you will continue to do to be effective with each high-leverage team action.

Green light: Indicate one activity you will begin to do immediately to become more effective with each high-leverage team action.

Figure 1.32: Setting your collaborative team's before-the-unit priorities.

Visit **go.solution-tree.com/mathematicsatwork** to download a reproducible version of this figure.

CHAPTER 2

During the Unit

The choice of classroom instruction and learning activities to maximize the outcome of surface knowledge and deeper processes is a hallmark of quality teaching.

—Mary Kennedy

Learning is experience. Everything else is just information.

—Albert Einstein

Much of the daily work of your collaborative team occurs during the unit of instruction. This makes sense, as it is during the unit that you place much of your collaborative team effort put forth before the unit into action.

Your team conversations during the unit focus on sharing evidence of student learning, discussing the effectiveness of lessons or activities, and examining the ways in which students may be challenged or need scaffolding to engage mathematically. While discussion about some of the tasks and the end-of-unit assessment planning take place prior to the start of the unit, teachers often plan and revise day-to-day unit lessons *during the unit* as they gain information regarding students' needs and successes. What your students do and say while developing understanding of the essential learning standards for the unit provides the data for your teacher team conversations.

This process of data gathering, sharing, providing feedback, and taking action regarding student learning forms the basis of an in-class *formative assessment process* throughout the unit. By sharing these efforts, your grade-level team can make needed adjustments in task development and instruction that will better support student learning during the unit. An effective formative assessment process also empowers students to make needed adjustments in their ways of thinking about and doing mathematics to lead to further learning.

This chapter is designed to help you and your collaborative team members prepare and organize your team's work and discussions around three high-leverage team actions during the unit of instruction. These three high-leverage actions support steps two and three of the PLC teaching-assessing-learning cycle in figure 2.1 (page 68).

The three high-leverage team actions that occur during the unit of instruction are:

> HLTA 6. Using higher-level-cognitive-demand mathematical tasks effectively
>
> HLTA 7. Using in-class formative assessment processes effectively
>
> HLTA 8. Using a lesson-design process for lesson planning and collective team inquiry

Steps two and three of the teaching-assessing-learning cycle provide a focus to your collaborative team's use of effective in-class lesson strategies as you support students' mathematics learning during the unit's instruction. How well your collaborative team implements formative feedback and assessment processes (step two) is only as effective as how well you and your team are able to elicit student actions and responses to the formative feedback you and their peers provide (step three). You can only effectively implement formative assessment if students are actively involved in the process.

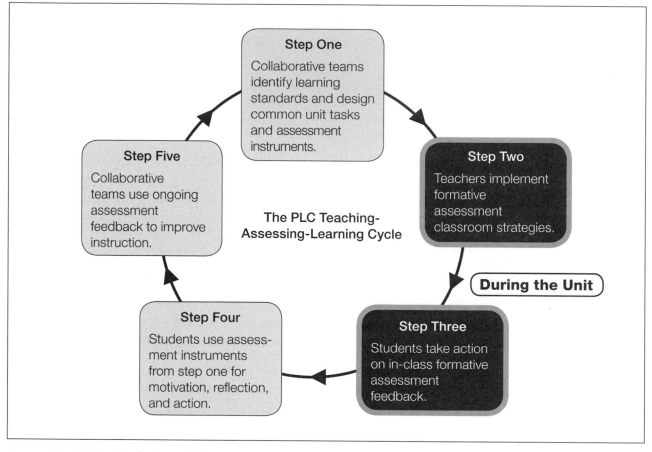

Source: Kanold, Kanold, & Larson, 2012.

Figure 2.1: Steps two and three of the PLC teaching-assessing-learning cycle.

As you begin your during-the-unit team discussions, set the stage by developing a common understanding of key terms you will use. You and your team should complete table 2.1 to organize your thinking prior to continuing through this chapter. Each team member will present common as well as different ways of thinking about teaching, assessing, and learning. A common understanding of the terms provides a foundation that facilitates thorough consideration of mathematics instruction to maximize student achievement. Once again, this work is about the constant and ongoing discussion between you and your team regarding knowing thy impact.

After each team member has responded to table 2.1, discuss how your team can use these key terms during the unit of instruction to bolster students' mathematics learning through collaborative team efforts. For example, some might include *student learning* in their definition of *teaching*, and others might not have considered that teaching does not truly occur unless a recipient of that teaching actually learns. This should lead to a discussion of how team members interpret the term *teaching*. You should revisit and consider understandings such as this as you work your way through this chapter. It is important to align your understandings of these terms to pursue an equitable formative assessment process.

Table 2.1: Common Understandings of Key Terms

Directions: Record your understandings of the following key terms. Provide an example to illustrate your understandings, and compare and contrast your understandings with other team members.		
Term	**Your Understanding**	**Example to Illustrate Your Understanding**
Teaching mathematics		
Assessing mathematics		
Learning mathematics		
Checking for understanding		
Using formative assessment processes		

Visit **go.solution-tree.com/mathematicsatwork** to download a reproducible version of this table.

As you focus attention on the Mathematical Practices and processes as an integral part of your instruction, the challenge is to envision these practices as student outcomes in the classroom. As you collaborate with your colleagues around instruction, your dialogue will focus specifically on the tasks you use, the questions you ask and students answer, the nature of your whole- and small-group discourse, and the way you manage the daily activities in which students participate. This should lead your team to consider the question, What are students doing as they engage in the Mathematical Practices?

The three high-leverage team actions in this chapter will allow you to go deeper in your use of higher-level-cognitive-demand tasks, implement the formative assessment process connected to the Mathematical Practices, and design lessons centered around K–5 learning standards and Mathematical Practices that include attention to both teacher and student actions. The Mathematical Practices lesson-planning tool discussed later in this chapter (see figure 2.21, page 108) provides one framework for synthesizing each of the three high-leverage team actions, moving your team closer to engagement in informal lesson study.

HLTA 6: Using Higher-Level-Cognitive-Demand Mathematical Tasks Effectively

The sixth high-leverage team action highlights the team's work to present, adjust, and use daily common higher- and lower-level-cognitive-demand mathematical tasks. These tasks were designed in step one of the teaching-assessing-learning cycle as part of the second HLTA (page 20).

The What

Recall there are four critical questions every collaborative team in a PLC culture asks and answers on an ongoing unit-by-unit basis.

1. What do we want all students to know and be able to do? (The essential learning standards)

2. How will we know if they know it? (The assessment instruments and tasks teams use)

3. How will we respond if they don't know it? (Formative assessment processes for intervention)

4. How will we respond if they do know it? (Formative assessment processes for extension and enrichment)

The sixth HLTA, using higher-level-cognitive-demand mathematical tasks effectively, ensures your team reaches clarity on the second PLC critical question, How will we know if they know it?

High-Leverage Team Action	1. What do we want all students to know and be able to do?	2. How will we know if they know it?	3. How will we respond if they don't know it?	4. How will we respond if they do know it?
During-the-Unit Action				
HLTA 6. Using higher-level-cognitive-demand mathematical tasks effectively	◧	▪		

◼ = Fully addressed with high-leverage team action

◧ = Partially addressed with high-leverage team action

You and your team intentionally plan for, design, and implement mathematical tasks that will provide student engagement and descriptive feedback around the elements of the learning objectives as well as standards for Mathematical Practices and processes. As mentioned in chapter 1, effective use of higher-level-cognitive-demand tasks also means that you do not lower the cognitive demand of the tasks implemented during instruction.

When students work on cognitively demanding tasks they often at first struggle. Some mathematics teachers too often perceive student struggle as an indicator that the teacher has failed instructionally. Thus, the teacher will jump in to rescue students by breaking down the task and guiding students step by step to a solution (Leinwand et al., 2014). This, in turn, deprives students of an opportunity to make sense of the mathematics (Stein, Remillard, & Smith, 2007) and does not support student engagement with Mathematical Practice 1—"Make sense of problems and persevere in solving them."

> Through your work on high-leverage team action 6, you help your students see that *productive struggle* is an important part of learning mathematics (Leinwand et al., 2014) and you begin to develop student proficiency in the Mathematical Practices and processes by using higher-level-cognitive-demand tasks in class that support learning the essential standards of the unit.

HLTA 6 consists of three action components:

1.   Understanding student proficiency in Mathematical Practices and processes

2.   Using higher-level-cognitive-demand tasks effectively during the unit of instruction

3.   Keeping a sustained focus on the essential learning standards during the unit of instruction

By placing your limited time and energy on these three teaching and learning components during the unit, you and your collaborative team can dissect this high-leverage team action and develop plans for making it a reality during instruction. The process begins by revisiting and exploring what is meant by student proficiency for the Standards for Mathematical Practice: practices that describe *how* students should engage with the mathematics during class. To review, the CCSS for mathematics provide eight Standards for Mathematical Practice. The eight Standards for Mathematical Practice (presented in more detail in appendix A, page 149) are (NGA & CCSSO, 2010, pp. 6–8):

1.   Make sense of problems and persevere in solving them.

2.   Reason abstractly and quantitatively.

3.   Construct viable arguments and critique the reasoning of others.

4.   Model with mathematics.

5.   Use appropriate tools strategically.

6.   Attend to precision.

7.   Look for and make use of structure.

8.   Look for and express regularity in repeated reasoning.

The How

To begin your work on this high-leverage team action, spend time deeply exploring each of the eight Mathematical Practices with your team. These standards represent important processes for student learning, whether your state is participating in the Common Core standards or not. In *Common Core Mathematics in a PLC at Work, Grades K–2* and *Grades 3–5* (Kanold, Larson, Fennell, Adams, Dixon, Kobett, & Wray, 2012a, 2012b), three key questions help you and your team better understand the Standards for Mathematical Practice.

> 1.   What is the intent of the Mathematical Practice, and why is it important?
>
> 2.   What teacher actions facilitate student engagement in this Mathematical Practice?
>
> 3.   What evidence is there that students are demonstrating this Mathematical Practice?

Each team member should be able to respond accurately and with depth to these three questions. Some ideas for your team to facilitate this process appear in the Mathematical Practice tool in table 2.2.

Table 2.2: In-Depth Study of the Standards for Mathematical Practice Tool

Directions: Choose one of the following assignments below and record your plans to carry out the assignment for studying the Mathematical Practices, and then record the outcome of the assignment.

Mathematical Practices Study Assignment	Plans to Carry Out Assignment	Outcome of the Assignment
Engage in a book study, using chapter 2 of *Common Core Mathematics in a PLC at Work, Grades K–2* (Kanold et al., 2012a) or *Common Core Mathematics in a PLC at Work, Grades 3–5* (Kanold et al., 2012b).	Sample plan: Each member of our team will read chapter 2 prior to our next collaborative team meeting. We will come to the meeting with a list of two things we learned, two actions we will take as a result of what we learned, and two questions that we need to discuss.	Sample outcome: Each team member participated and felt that his or her instruction was influenced by what was read. Sharing activities was helpful in coming up with new ways to support student engagement with the Mathematical Practices. We were able to answer questions brought by our team members.
Develop scenarios from your instruction, and discuss ways to increase focus on the Mathematical Practices that will positively impact students' learning.		
Select a Mathematical Practice, and locate a journal article that describes the practice conceptually or represents the practice in action. Discuss the article as a collaborative team.		

Visit **go.solution-tree.com/mathematicsatwork** to download a reproducible version of this table.

In addition to completing one of the assignments in table 2.2 with your team, use the adaptation of the Frayer model as an effective technique to investigate the intent and reasoning behind each Mathematical Practice. (See figure 2.2, page 74.) This model provides a useful framework to unpack the meaning of the Mathematical Practices with a focus on classroom implementation. You and your collaborative team should work through each of the eight practices one at a time to create posters (electronically or with poster paper) using the Frayer model. Post these in your teacher work area as a reminder of student expectations for demonstrating each Mathematical Practice. What does each practice look like and sound like in your classroom? That is, what should you expect to see and hear from your students when they are doing mathematics in your classroom?

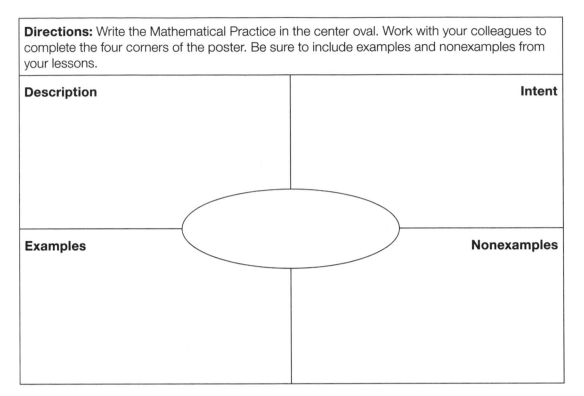

Directions: Write the Mathematical Practice in the center oval. Work with your colleagues to complete the four corners of the poster. Be sure to include examples and nonexamples from your lessons.

Description	Intent
Examples	Nonexamples

Source: Adapted from Frayer, Frederick, & Klausmeier, 1969.

Figure 2.2: Using the Frayer model for Mathematical Practices.

Since the Mathematical Practices represent what students are to do, one of your first responsibilities is to expect students to demonstrate their understanding of each process standard as the year progresses. Your second responsibility is to ensure students experience mathematical tasks or activities that allow them to actually demonstrate the Standard for Mathematical Practice as part of your lesson planning for each unit.

Likely, your examples and nonexamples will reflect what you currently see, or plan to see, in your classroom around each Mathematical Practice. For example, a Frayer model poster for Mathematical Practice 5, "Use appropriate tools strategically" might have information related to the following for its description, intent, examples, and nonexamples:

- **Description**—Students know what tools are useful for given problems and use those tools in ways to increase efficiency and understanding. Students know the benefits of using one tool over another for a given problem context and discern appropriately when to use different tools.

- **Intent**—Students have access to a wide variety of tools. The tools students choose provide data in the formative assessment process related to how students think about the problem.

- **Example**—Second-grade students choose base ten blocks to solve a multidigit addition problem that involves regrouping but use an open number line to solve an addition problem where the first addend is two digits and the second is one digit.

- **Nonexample**—The teacher directs the students to use base ten blocks to solve all multidigit addition problems.

Discuss your team's examples and nonexamples from the Frayer model activity to determine if all of the described actions in the examples are present in your classrooms and what teachers can do to make them more common. The example describes what student proficiency in a Mathematical Practice might look like. You can use the ideas from your team discussion as a basis for understanding how to capture student proficiency.

Understanding Student Proficiency in the Mathematical Practices

It is important to note that your team's investigation of the Mathematical Practices is all about understanding how students are to *learn and do* mathematics. As a reader and user of this handbook, whether or not your state adopted the Common Core, is a member of one of the Common Core assessment consortia, or has established singular state standards and assessments, is not essential to this high-leverage action. Research about how students learn mathematics at high levels of achievement is the basis on which the Mathematical Practices and processes stand (Hattie, 2012; Kilpatrick, Swafford, & Findell, 2001; NCTM, 2014). In short, your deep understanding of how to develop student proficiency in these practices has a considerable learning benefit to the student. (See appendix C on page 155 or visit **go.solution-tree .com/mathematicsatwork** to access research resources related to the ten high-leverage team actions in this handbook.)

Student proficiency with the Mathematical Practices must involve both conceptual and procedural understandings of mathematics. Most likely, the level of student proficiency will vary for many reasons. For example, what proficiency looks like for a kindergarten student will be different from what proficiency looks like for a fifth-grade student. Proficiency will also vary across topics within a grade. For example, topics within the fourth-grade standards in the domains Number and Operations in Base Ten (4.OA) versus Geometry (4.G) will warrant different types of proficiency (see NGA & CCSSO, 2010, pp. 29, 32).

You and your colleagues will need to develop consensus on the meaning of *proficiency* relative to students' engagement with the Mathematical Practices. To support this work, use figure 2.3 (page 76) to organize your collaborative team's initial ideas about proficiency and the Mathematical Practices. It will be helpful to return to the source of the Standards for Mathematical Practice. You should take caution if using posters available online to make sense of the standards as they are often oversimplified and based on interpretations of the Mathematical Practices that may not be true to the source. The original descriptions of the Standards for Mathematical Practice are provided in appendix A (page 149).

Students' proficiency with the Mathematical Practices will be apparent through effective class discussion and instruction around both lower- and higher-level-cognitive-demand mathematical tasks. The lower-level-cognitive-demand mathematical tasks might involve teacher-student dialogue; however, the higher-level-cognitive-demand mathematical tasks must include student-to-student discussions around the tasks.

Directions: Record your insights about proficiency with the Standards for Mathematical Practice.
Mathematical Practice 1: When students are proficient with making sense of problems and persevering in solving them, they . . .
Mathematical Practice 2: When students are proficient with reasoning abstractly and quantitatively, they . . .
Mathematical Practice 3: When students are proficient with constructing viable arguments and critiquing the reasoning of others, they . . .
Mathematical Practice 4: When students are proficient with modeling with mathematics, they . . .
Mathematical Practice 5: When students are proficient with using appropriate tools strategically, they . . .
Mathematical Practice 6: When students are proficient with attending to precision, they . . .
Mathematical Practice 7: When students are proficient with looking for and making use of structure, they . . .
Mathematical Practice 8: When students are proficient with looking for and expressing regularity in repeated reasoning, they . . .

Figure 2.3: Identifying proficiency with the Standards for Mathematical Practice.

Visit **go.solution-tree.com/mathematicsatwork** to download a reproducible version of this figure.

Using Higher-Level-Cognitive-Demand Tasks Effectively During the Unit of Instruction

Consider the scenario in figure 2.4 (page 78). This scenario describes the thinking of a teacher using a task she planned with her grade-level team. With your team, respond to the questions after you read the scenario.

Your effective use of higher-level-cognitive-demand mathematical tasks during the unit of instruction (to develop student reasoning and problem-solving ability) will benefit from team discussions of topics such as those in figure 2.4. During the unit, each team member should bring a higher-level-cognitive-demand mathematical task to the team meeting. The task can be teacher developed or from a resource, but it should be one the teacher identified as part of the second high-leverage team action from chapter 1—identifying higher-level-cognitive-demand mathematical tasks. The questions used to explore the football task in figure 2.4 are helpful in preparing to implement other higher-level-cognitive-demand mathematical tasks. During the meeting, use the prompts in figure 2.5 (page 79) to promote deep discussion of each task.

A closer examination of Mathematical Practice 1—"Make sense of problems and persevere in solving them"—provides a context for higher-level-cognitive-demand mathematical task development during the unit of instruction.

For Mathematical Practice 1, the expectation is that students will encounter problem situations in the form of mathematical tasks that will stretch them in a mathematical sense. They will experience *productive struggle* together during a task—that is, a struggle that moves learning forward rather than just a struggle that leads to frustration and disappointment. The intent is for students to face challenge without an easily understood solution pathway. A challenge for you and your collaborative team is to determine specific strategies for your students so that they are engaged in productive struggle.

It is tempting to step in and offer assistance or to solve the problem for struggling students. A better response is to provide scaffolding prompts for the task so that the struggle is productive rather than to lower the task's cognitive demand.

To develop students' proficiency with making sense of problems and persevering in solving them, you and your team need to provide good higher-level-cognitive-demand mathematical tasks, helpful resources, and targeted and differentiated support during instruction to maintain the task's demand. As an example for thinking through these three components, consider the grade 4 problem-solving higher-level-cognitive-demand mathematical task in figure 2.6 (page 80).

First, consider whether or not this problem is a good higher-level-cognitive-demand mathematical task. Remember from chapter 1 (page 23) that good higher-level-cognitive-demand mathematical tasks provide opportunities for students to reason about mathematics and to connect procedures to their conceptual foundations. Teachers need to plan for students to access prior knowledge as well as for opportunities to develop new knowledge. The task in figure 2.6 assumes students know attributes of triangles and can connect to their prior knowledge of six types of triangles—three classified by lengths of their sides and three classified by measures of their angles.

Directions: Read the scenario, and answer the questions that follow.

Mary Mostessi enters her grade 4 class prepared to engage her students in an active learning experience. She planned the unit with her grade-level collaborative team, and she is excited about sharing her and her students' experiences with the team. A few of her team members were able to come to her class and observe students during the lesson. After her students are settled into class, she presents the following task.

> Michael watched his favorite football team play a game on television. During the game, however, he had to complete a chore for his father. Because he had to do the chore, he missed the times when his team scored. His team did win, and he knows that the final score for his team was 47. The possible ways of scoring are touchdowns (6 points each), field goals (3 points each), safeties (2 points each), two-point conversions (2 points each), and extra points (1 point each). According to the rules of football, how might have Michael's team scored its points? Explain.

1. Ms. Mostessi and her team selected this task because they thought it would engage students. What do you suppose the teachers considered engaging about the task?

2. How would you modify the task to increase its potential to engage students?

3. What is the targeted learning standard for this task?

4. What other real-life topic might be useful as a context for the same mathematics in the task?

5. What can you learn about students as they engage in and respond to this task?

6. What do you expect students' wonderings and questions to be regarding the task?

7. What do you expect students' misunderstandings to be regarding the task?

8. What might make the mathematics of the task less or more challenging to meet the needs of students?

9. Because student responses to the mathematical task will vary, how do you propose to facilitate assessment of the task?

Figure 2.4: Mathematics instruction and higher-level-cognitive-demand mathematical task scenario.

Visit **go.solution-tree.com/mathematicsatwork** to download a reproducible version of this figure.

Directions: Use these questions to allow for deep discussion of each higher-level-cognitive-demand mathematical task.

1. Why did you select or create this task?

2. How would you modify the task to increase its potential to engage students?

3. What is the targeted learning standard for this task?

4. What is the real-life topic of this task? What other real-life topic might be useful as a context for the same mathematics in the task?

5. What can you learn about students as they engage in and respond to the task?

6. How might you provide scaffolding to a student who struggles without lowering the cognitive demand of the task too much?

7. What do you expect students' wonderings and questions to be regarding the task?

8. What do you expect students' misunderstandings to be regarding the task?

9. What might make the mathematics of the task less or more challenging to meet the needs of students?

10. How do you propose assessment of the task should be effectively managed and facilitated?

Figure 2.5: Mathematics instruction and higher-level-cognitive-demand mathematical task development tool.

Visit **go.solution-tree.com/mathematicsatwork** to download a reproducible version of this figure.

Directions: Which triangle combinations are possible to construct? If possible, sketch an example of the triangle. If a triangle combination is not possible, explain. (See 4.G.1 and 4.G.2.)

	Obtuse	Acute	Right
Equilateral			
Isosceles			
Scalene			

Figure 2.6: Grade 4 problem-solving higher-level-cognitive-demand mathematical task.

Visit **go.solution-tree.com/mathematicsatwork** to download a reproducible version of this figure.

For this task, students will be able to use their knowledge of these types of triangles to develop an understanding of how side lengths and angle measures of triangles interact with one another. The task provides the opportunity for students to ponder, hypothesize, discuss, and debate. Use probing questions to help guide students in the process of exploring the mathematical task, such as:

- What do you know about [insert name of triangle] triangles?

- Show me a triangle. [Give students time to do this.] How can you name the triangle? What other name could you use for this triangle?

- Draw several different examples of [insert name of triangle] triangles. What is the same about them? What is different about them?

Effective higher-level-cognitive-demand mathematical tasks provide an opportunity for students to showcase their learning in multiple ways. For example, if students worked on this particular task in small groups, each group member could take on the responsibility of developing and testing the hypothesis for one or two cases presented in the problem. Other students might sketch drawings, while other students might develop justifications for triangle combinations that are not possible. This is one teaching strategy you could use in your lesson design to support the implementation of higher-level-cognitive-demand tasks and ensure students have the opportunity to develop their proficiency with Mathematical Practice 1—"Make sense of problems and persevere in solving them."

In addition, for students to engage in problem-solving tasks that build proficiency and support students in making sense of problems and persevering in solving them, students need access to helpful resources. Consider using a tool such as figure 2.7 to select, locate, and organize resources for this purpose. Resources should be available during instruction to support tasks like the one in figure 2.6. The sample items in figure 2.7 correspond with the task in figure 2.6.

Directions: Complete the table to select, locate, and organize instructional resources.		
Possible Resources	**Where Can We Find the Selected Resources?**	**How Should We Organize the Resources?**
Geoboards and Geoboard dot paper	Media center	Three Geoboards in each table group kit
AngLegs	Media center	One pack for each table group
The Geometer's Sketchpad (www .dynamicgeometry.com) or GeoGebra (www.geogebra.org)	Computer lab	Computer lab and student pairs

Figure 2.7: Selecting, locating, and organizing resources tool.

Visit **go.solution-tree.com/mathematicsatwork** to download a reproducible version of this figure.

Two possible resources for this task are Geoboards and Geoboard dot paper. Teams can find these resources on school supply company websites, as resources within an adopted textbook or kit, or as virtual manipulatives in a technology-rich classroom. In regard to organization, each small group can share a Geoboard, or each student can use a Geoboard and Geoboard dot paper for recording his or her findings. Discussing these and other possibilities for managing the task is a helpful way to decide the best resources for supporting students' engagement in higher-level-cognitive-demand mathematical tasks.

Finally, to empower students to benefit from a higher-level-cognitive-demand mathematical task, and to subsequently develop proficiency in the practice of learning mathematics (such as with Mathematical Practice 1), you must provide students with targeted and differentiated in-class support. You need to guide and facilitate the in-class problem-solving experience. There are many actions you can take to provide such support. Consider the teacher actions for targeted and differentiated support in figure 2.8 (page 82) as part of your required and ongoing classroom practice.

Engaging in discussions about targeted and differentiated support during higher-level-cognitive-demand mathematical tasks will help you and your collaborative team avoid the temptation to *teach by telling*. When higher-level-cognitive-demand mathematical tasks are taught by telling—through direct instruction with the teacher modeling each step of the problem—it is unlikely that the cognitive demand is maintained.

Strategies for providing targeted and differentiated task support include the following:
• Engage in higher-level-cognitive-demand mathematical tasks with students so that students can observe effective and expected problem-solving behavior. Your students need constant feedback from you and from each other during the learning experience.
• Encourage students to persist on a task, scaffolding as needed to support students' learning. Remember your personal classroom goal is not student struggle but student productive struggle.
• Pull from a pool of carefully selected hints or scaffolding prompts for higher-level-cognitive-demand mathematical tasks so that students can receive support to respond to a task without being given so much information that they do not need to put forth much effort.
• Help students notice the progressions of structures in the mathematics content, such as when they use strategies based on properties of operations to multiply. This will help them better recognize types of differences and similarities between mathematical situations.

Figure 2.8: Teacher actions that provide targeted and differentiated support.

Visit **go.solution-tree.com/mathematicsatwork** to download a reproducible version of this figure.

Keeping a Sustained Focus on the Essential Learning Standards During the Unit of Instruction

Research indicates that "the higher the cognitive demands of the tasks at the set-up phase, the lower the percentage of tasks that actually remained that way during implementation" (Smith, Grover, & Henningsen, 1996, p. 476). This indicates that higher-level-cognitive-demand mathematical tasks are likely to be reduced to lower-level-cognitive-demand mathematical tasks during instruction, if you are not careful. This occurs when you shift into a teach-by-telling mode of instruction. To help you plan for the expectations in figure 2.8, use the prompts in figure 2.9. Figure 2.9 provides a platform for you and your colleagues to discuss ways each team member can provide targeted support for students to successfully develop proficiency and persevere with problem solving.

Sometimes students just need encouragement to persevere. Careful observations and engagement with your students during problem solving will help you determine when this is needed. Carol Dweck's (2007) research provides critical insight into the nature of your praise. Students will be increasingly more apt to persevere through more challenging mathematical tasks when the nature of the praise they receive from you rewards their effort and not their ability. For example, you might say, "I like how you are making many different triangles with the angle manipulative to explore whether a scalene triangle can be acute." This praise focuses on the student's specific effort rather than focusing on the student's ability if you say, "You are so smart!"

Forward thinking about providing targeted and differentiated support on the tasks you use during the unit of instruction is an effective means of ensuring that each team member is equipped with strategies to guide students in the learning process. This is also a great place for team discussions on how students are progressing overall during the unit. Are there collective and collaborative actions your team can take to provide intervention and enrichment to all students in your grade level during the unit? Figure 2.10 (page 84) shows some strategies for maintaining higher-level cognitive demand of tasks during instruction.

Directions: Within your collaborative team, complete each statement by providing one or two indicators for targeted and differentiated support for students to engage in higher-level-cognitive-demand mathematical tasks.

1. My class allows students to take risks when engaging in higher-level-cognitive-demand mathematical tasks because . . .

2. Students know I have high expectations for their development and perseverance as good problem solvers because . . .

3. The types of questions that build students' proficiency, perseverance, and endurance with problem solving are . . .

4. When students are stuck on a problem . . .

   + I do this . . .

   + They do this . . .

5. My assessment of students' progress in developing their problem-solving skills is meant to . . .

6. If students need a resource when engaging with a problem-solving task, they . . .

7. Students know that when it comes to problem solving in class, I . . .

Figure 2.9: Prompts for targeted and differentiated in-class support.

Visit **go.solution-tree.com/mathematicsatwork** to download a reproducible version of this figure.

Strategies for maintaining higher-level cognitive demand during instruction include:

- **Monitoring students' initial responses to problems**—If students indicate the task is easy, then the task most likely does not rise to the level of higher-level cognitive demand for those students.

- **Presenting tasks in a way that requires students to apply mathematical knowledge and skills**—The goal is for students to translate their mathematical understandings from one context to another as one indicator of mathematical proficiency.

- **Expecting students to provide counterexamples and compare and contrast mathematical concepts**—Tasks shouldn't just focus on asking students to provide examples of mathematical concepts.

- **Engaging students in solving problems orally**—Encourage the important and proper use of mathematical terminology and logical sequence of processes.

Figure 2.10: Strategies for maintaining higher-level cognitive demand for tasks during instruction.

Visit **go.solution-tree.com/mathematicsatwork** to download a reproducible version of this figure.

Developing student proficiency with each of the Standards for Mathematical Practice through the use of higher-level-cognitive-demand mathematical tasks is possible when your team has a good understanding of each Mathematical Practice, has reached agreement on proficiency with each Mathematical Practice, and is committed to maintaining a level of high cognitive demand during instruction. However, it is equally important to ensure your students understand how the task is aligned and representative of the essential learning standard for the unit.

Student proficiency in each Mathematical Practice through the use of higher-level cognitive demand tasks is a vehicle that leads to student understanding of the learning standard; otherwise, tasks are simply random problems for the student to solve.

Recall your discussion in chapter 1 regarding strategies for finding 6×7. Your team's effort to unpack the learning standard was a precursor for understanding what is desired of students' learning experiences regarding multiplication. During instruction, you and your team can make inferences from students' engagement about the level of proficiency students are developing in select Mathematical Practices.

For instance, for Mathematical Practice 7—"Look for and make use of structure"—consider the following three events during instruction.

1. Students are using knowledge of related multiplication facts (such as 6×6).

2. Students indicate notice of the change that takes place from 6×6 to 6×7 (such as adding one more to each of the six groups, so there are six groups of seven rather than six groups of six).

3. Students demonstrate understanding of the mathematical structure via drawings or manipulatives.

These students made use of structure by relating the fact strategy of using a known fact, like 6×6, to find a fact that is not known to them, like 6×7, but then described how the two facts are related. They used drawings or manipulatives to explicate that structure. This is an appropriate example of engagement in Mathematical Practice 7 that can be determined through observation. You are more likely to observe this engagement if you highlight an expectation for it during planning.

In particular, your team benefits during the unit from the deep discussions you had before instruction began. Thus, how students might engage with the mathematics and demonstrate their learning *during* instruction becomes a routine part of your work together.

Your Team's Progress

As you and your team focus on using higher-level-cognitive-demand mathematical tasks effectively for student learning through demonstrations of Mathematical Practices and processes, reflect on your perspectives related to this pursuit. Your team members should individually assess the team using the status check tool in table 2.3 (page 86) to determine how well your collaborative team is currently pursuing the sixth high-leverage team action. Discuss your team's progress on using higher-level-cognitive-demand mathematical tasks effectively.

Remember that learning *how* is as important as learning *what* for students, and learning how manifests itself in the many decisions you make every day around the robust and intentional use of in-class formative assessment. This is the focus of the seventh high-leverage team action.

Table 2.3: During-the-Unit Status Check Tool for HLTA 6—Using Higher-Level-Cognitive-Demand Mathematical Tasks Effectively

Directions: Discuss your perception of your team's progress on the sixth high-leverage team action—using higher-level-cognitive-demand mathematical tasks effectively. Defend your reasoning.			
Stage I: Pre-Initiating	**Stage II: Initiating**	**Stage III: Developing**	**Stage IV: Sustaining**
We do not attend to or discuss Mathematical Practices or processes.	We have discussed Mathematical Practices and processes.	We consistently discuss the intent, purpose, and evidence of Mathematical Practices and processes during each unit of study.	We engage, as a team, in deep planning for Mathematical Practices and processes in our lessons.
We do not have a clear understanding of each Mathematical Practice.	We do not have a collaborative agreement on the focus of the Mathematical Practices for each unit of the course.	We teach some aspect of various Mathematical Practices as part of every daily lesson.	We use higher-level-cognitive-demand tasks as an intended activity to meet both the essential learning standards and the Mathematical Practices outlined for the lesson and the unit.
We do not use common higher-level-cognitive-demand tasks in order to develop students' Mathematical Practices.	We discuss and use some common higher-level-cognitive-demand tasks in class.	We discuss and implement collaboratively developed higher-level-cognitive-demand tasks.	We discuss and use intentional and targeted differentiated in-class supports as students engage in the Mathematical Practices by using our common and higher-level-cognitive-demand mathematical tasks.
We do not know the Mathematical Practices expected or demonstrated by the students assigned to other members of our team.	We have not reached team agreement on how to implement and sustain student proficiency in the Mathematical Practice expectations.	We do not collaboratively plan for Mathematical Practices, and they do not influence daily instructional plans for the unit.	We collaboratively plan for and implement Mathematical Practices and processes as part of our daily instructional plans for the unit.

Visit **go.solution-tree.com/mathematicsatwork** to download a reproducible version of this table.

HLTA 7: Using In-Class Formative Assessment Processes Effectively

[Formative assessment] can essentially double the speed of student learning producing large gains in students' achievement.

—James Popham

Recall there are four critical questions every collaborative team in a PLC asks and answers on a unit-by-unit, ongoing basis.

1. What do we want all students to know and be able to do? (The essential learning standards)

2. How will we know if they know it? (The assessment instruments and tasks teams use)

3. How will we respond if they don't know it? (Formative assessment processes for intervention)

4. How will we respond if they do know it? (Formative assessment processes for extension and enrichment)

The seventh high-leverage team action—using in-class formative assessment processes effectively—ensures you and your collaborative team reach clarity on how to effectively respond in class to the third and fourth critical questions of a PLC, How will we respond if they don't know it? How will we respond if they do know it?

High-Leverage Team Action	1. What do we want all students to know and be able to do?	2. How will we know if they know it?	3. How will we respond if they don't know it?	4. How will we respond if they do know it?
During-the-Unit Action				
HLTA 7. Using in-class formative assessment processes effectively	◨	◨	▢	▢

◼ = Fully addressed with high-leverage team action

◨ = Partially addressed with high-leverage team action

Through your work on this high-leverage team action, you will begin to develop student proficiency in each of the Mathematical Practices as well as other processes of student learning through engaging lessons. Descriptive feedback will also guide student actions toward achieving the learning standards and the Mathematical Practice targets for that lesson.

The What

The formative assessment process involves the following components: unpacking the essential learning content and practice standards (see chapter 1, page 11), developing and using well-designed common assessment tasks or instruments (see chapter 1, page 33), collecting data through the implementation of those tasks and assessment instruments in class, providing clear and descriptive feedback to students, and using the feedback (students and teachers) to adjust teaching and learning. For the feedback process to be formative, the students and the teacher must take action on the feedback.

High-leverage team action 7 calls for students to develop proficiency in Mathematical Practices and processes through the use of effective formative assessment procedures led by you during instruction. Typically, one might not think of assessment as a support for learning, but effective assessment (particularly the formative assessment process) is at the core of the PLC teaching-assessing-learning cycle (figure 2.1, page 68).

According to Dylan Wiliam (2011):

> When formative assessment practices are integrated into the minute-to-minute and day-by-day classroom activities of teachers, substantial increases in student achievement—of the order of a 70 to 80% increase in the speed of learning are possible. . . . Moreover, these changes are not expensive to produce. . . . The currently available evidence suggests that there is nothing else remotely affordable that is likely to have such a large effect. (p. 161)

You and your collaborative team should not ignore this wise advice. Used effectively, this high-leverage action will have a substantial and positive impact on your students' learning. This is what Hattie (2012) means when he says, "Teacher, know thy impact" (p. ix).

During the unit of instruction, part of your team's work is to discuss how to build your confidence for using in-class formative assessment processes. This is much more than just observing evidence of student learning (checking for understanding), which is, at best, diagnostic. For the process to also be formative, you, your students' peers, or both must provide meaningful and formative feedback during engagement with mathematics tasks and problems.

According to Reeves (2011) and Hattie (2009, 2012), there are four markers that provide a basis for effective formative feedback to your students. We have organized these markers into the acronym FAST:

1. **Feedback must be Fair:** Does your feedback rest solely on the quality of student work and not on other characteristics of the student, including some form of comparison to others in the classroom?

2. **Feedback must be Accurate:** Is the feedback during the in-class activity actually correct? Do students receive prompts, solution pathway suggestions, and discourse that are effective for understanding the mathematical task as you tour the room observing students during peer-to-peer discourse, checking for understanding, and providing feedback?

3. **Feedback must be Specific:** Does the verbal feedback students receive contain enough specificity to help them persevere and stay engaged in the mathematical task or activity process? Does the feedback help students to get "unstuck" or to advance their thinking as needed? (For example, "Work harder on the problem" is not helpful feedback for a student.)

4. **Feedback must be Timely:** As you tour the room, observe students during peer-to-peer discourse, and listen in on the peer-to-peer conversations, is your feedback immediate and corrective to keep students on track for the solution pathway?

However, FAST meaningful feedback from you and from student peers alone is not sufficient for student learning. If, during the best teacher-designed moments of classroom formative assessment processes, teachers fail to support students *taking action* on areas of difficulty (step three of the PLC teaching-assessing-learning cycle, page 68), then the cycle of learning, assessing, and continued learning, stops for the student (Wiliam, 2011).

The How

According to James Popham (2011), when teachers use formative assessment well:

> It can essentially double the speed of student learning producing large gains in students' achievement; and at the same time, it is sufficiently robust so different teachers can use it in diverse ways and still get great results with their students. (p. 36)

So what does this have to do with the work of your collaborative team? Your work should begin with making sure your team is clear about the often used (and misused) in-class teaching technique of checking for understanding.

Checking for Understanding Versus Using Formative Assessment Processes

You and your colleagues need to be clear about the difference between solely checking for understanding in class (which has minimal impact on student learning) and using formative assessment processes (which includes the classroom elements of formative feedback and student action on feedback). Think back to table 2.1 (page 68) and your responses to the definitions of these concepts. To facilitate your discussion of these differences, engage with your team in the formative assessment process tool in figure 2.11 (page 90).

Directions: Answer the following questions.

1. How do you currently check for student understanding on a daily basis? Write your responses in the Checking for Understanding column. For each response, indicate whether you use whole-group discourse (teaching at the front of the room) with a *W*, small-group discourse (students working with their peers) with an *S*, independent practice (students working individually) with an *I*, or *M* for multiple formats.

2. What do you and your colleagues believe is the difference between solely checking for understanding and using formative assessment processes in the classroom during instruction?

3. How can you implement formative assessment processes in the classroom each day?

Remember, for the process to be formative, students must actually take action on the feedback they receive. In the Using Formative Assessment Processes column, explain ways that you could improve each check for understanding you listed to become a moment of formative assessment for your students.

Checking for Understanding	Using Formative Assessment Processes

Circle one: **W S I M**

Figure 2.11: Checking for understanding versus using the formative assessment process tool.

Visit **go.solution-tree.com/mathematicsatwork** *to download a reproducible version of this figure.*

As you learn more about how to engage in this high-leverage team action, you can add to your responses in figure 2.11. You promote conceptual understanding when you explicitly make, or ask students to make, connections among ideas, facts, and procedures (Hiebert & Grouws, 2007). The following four actions help students make these connections (Kanold, Briars, & Fennell, 2012).

1. Challenging students to think and to make sense of what they are doing to solve mathematics problems

2. Posing questions that stimulate students' thinking and reasoning—asking them to justify their conclusions, solution strategies, and procedures

3. Expecting students to evaluate and explain the work of other students and compare and contrast different solution methods for the same problem

4. Asking students to represent the same ideas in multiple ways—using multiple representations, such as symbols, graphics, or manipulatives to demonstrate a concept

What does a robust formative assessment process look like in the classroom? Consider figure 2.12 (page 92). In figure 2.12, you and your team revisit the scenario from figure 2.4 (page 78) and examine key formative assessment process questions to consider as part of the task. You should take the time together to respond to the questions accompanying the scenario.

At the heart of a robust vision for mathematics instruction is what your students are *doing* during class. How are they engaged? With whom are the most noteworthy conversations taking place in your classroom: student-to-student or teacher-to-student? Moreover, in your classroom, do your students see each other as reliable and valuable resources for learning?

The Mathematical Practices and processes, and good mathematics instruction in general, are best implemented via small-group discourse, providing opportunities for both teachers and peers to offer formative feedback to each other during class. However, for feedback to be effective, students must take action on the formative feedback they receive.

Going beyond checking for understanding from the front of the classroom and moving into using meaningful formative feedback as part of instruction require well-managed activities as you orchestrate all types of advancing and assessing prompts—allowing student-engaged exploration and discussion with peers. Much of this will occur out among the students as you become a facilitator of instruction rather than being a teller of information, or within small groups of students.

Work in your team with figure 2.13 (page 93) to revisit the tasks from chapter 1 (figure 1.7, page 24) that most closely relate to your team's grade-level responsibilities. Use your responses from figure 2.13 to help you determine scaffolding and enrichment prompts you could use for each task—specifically, what questions might you ask of students to keep them engaged in each task? What particular student solution strategies or activities (interventions) should you use as you observe and provide feedback to students as they engage in each task?

Directions: Revisit the scenario from figure 2.4 (page 78). Respond to the formative assessment process questions.

Mary Mostessi recalls that the last time she used the following problem-solving task in a lesson, she needed to be more prepared to determine what students were or were not learning as they engaged in the task. This time, during instruction, she is committed to gathering student learning data to make better decisions about the type of formative feedback to provide and the next steps in instruction and student action to increase the potential for student learning.

> Michael watched his favorite football team play a game on television. During the game, however, he had to complete a chore for his father. Because he had to do the chore, he missed the times when his team scored. His team did win, and he knows that the final score for his team was 47. The possible ways of scoring are: touchdowns (6 points each), field goals (3 points each), safeties (2 points each), two-point conversions (2 points each), and extra points (1 point each). According to the rules of football, how might have Michael's team scored its points? Explain.

1. Ms. Mostessi wants to probe her students' thinking with a series of questions. Following are two question starters. Suggest two more question starters.

   + How does a team score in football?

   + About how many times can a team score in football?

2. What questions do you anticipate the students will ask Ms. Mostessi?

3. Ms. Mostessi observed several students counting by three, counting by six, and counting by seven. What can she infer about these particular student actions?

4. Which problem-solving strategies (such as working backward) might Ms. Mostessi observe the students engaging in?

5. Because student responses to the task will vary, how should Ms. Mostessi facilitate the formative assessment process for the task? What type of prompts and scaffolding interventions might you use for students or student teams that are stuck?

6. What misconceptions do you anticipate Ms. Mostessi will uncover? What suggestions do you have to help her address these misconceptions?

Figure 2.12: Mathematics instruction scenario revisited.

Visit **go.solution-tree.com/mathematicsatwork** to download a reproducible version of this figure.

Directions: Within your team, revisit the tasks from chapter 1 in figure 1.7 (page 24). Work through each task, and discuss the results (such as students' solution strategies, questions students pose, and so on) that might emerge as students experience the task.

Also, discuss the type of interventions (scaffolding prompts) and enrichment (advancing questions) you might need to support the use of the task in class.

Task for Grade K (K.CC.6)

Blake has a number of cubes that is 1 more than 15. Jessica has a number of cubes that is 1 less than 17. Who has more cubes? How do you know?

Task for Grade 1 (1.G.3)

Calvin is at a birthday party where children will be sitting at tables. The chairs are already set up at each table. At one table, there are two chairs, and a mini birthday cake that is cut in halves. At another table, there are four chairs, and a mini birthday cake of the same size cut in fourths.

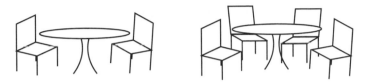

Calvin thinks that he will get the same amount of cake wherever he sits because he will get a piece of birthday cake no matter what. Tell if you agree or disagree, and say why.

Task for Grade 2 (2.NBT.5)

Alex was partway finished with a problem in mathematics class in which she needed to find $48 + 25$ when it was time to leave for lunch. The teacher picked up Alex's paper and was not sure if Alex was correct. Describe how Alex could be correct as well as the last step she still had to complete.

$$48 + 25$$
$$40 + 20 = 60$$
$$8 + 2 = 10$$
$$60 + 10 = 70$$

Task for Grade 3 (3.OA.4)

A student in your class is asked to solve 6×7 without drawing pictures. The student does not know the fact. Provide two different ways the student could use multiplication to solve the fact by using other facts the student might know.

Task for Grade 4 (4.OA.2)

Write four different story problems to correspond to the following expression: $46 \div 4$. Each problem should lead to a different answer. The answers to the problems should be 11½, 12, 11, and 2. Do not use the words *estimate*, *about*, or *round* in your problems.

Task for Grade 5 (5.NF.4a and 5.NF.6)

Write a word problem for ⅔ × ¾, then use a visual model to solve it that is supportive of the context used in your word problem.

Figure 2.13: Grade-level tasks revisited for formative assessment feedback and action considerations.

Visit **go.solution-tree.com/mathematicsatwork** to download a reproducible version of this figure.

The Heart of Formative Assessment: Developing In-Class Student Reasoning, Discourse, and Engagement Using Differentiation of Tasks

Consider Mathematical Practice 2—"Reason abstractly and quantitatively." One of the primary expectations of the K–5 standards is to provide students with learning experiences for reasoning. One topic in which opportunities for student reasoning abound is the essential learning standards for numbers. Given that *number* is a foundational concept for mathematics, it is essential that students come to know and be able to use number concepts to make sense and reason within and outside of mathematics. Young students, such as those in kindergarten, will develop a strong sense of number in preparation for further growth in mathematics.

What does it mean to reason? Your answers to this question will help determine the kinds of mathematical experiences you provide students and how you assess their understanding in the contexts of these experiences. Consider the first-grade higher-level-cognitive-demand mathematical task for reasoning in figure 2.14.

While using higher-level-cognitive-demand mathematical tasks such as the one in figure 2.14 during instruction, your team will need to engage in various formative assessment strategies. For example, oral assessment, either addressing each student with one question at a time or asking multiple questions to the same student, can uncover depth of student thinking. You can do this through whole-group discourse or in a small group with student-to-student discussion.

Consider the formative assessment process tool in figure 2.15 (page 96). As you pose the task and walk around the room, you are observing students working on the first-grade higher-level-cognitive-demand mathematical task for reasoning from figure 2.14, asking prompting questions, providing students with meaningful feedback, and expecting them to take action on your feedback. You collect information about the results of student engagement with the activity. During this formative process, you provide guidance and scaffold questions to support student learning and perseverance on the task. You also determine if you need to make adjustments in your whole-group instruction to develop students' reasoning skills. This is part of your ongoing form of intervention and support for the essential learning standards for that day.

You and your team should discuss how this tool or a modification of it (such as student teams versus individual students) might be useful in providing information about students' development of proficiency to reason abstractly and quantitatively during your lessons.

It is important to support student proficiency with *all* of the Mathematical Practices through the use of a formative assessment process during instruction. A key to success with this process is to make your plans to implement effective formative assessment strategies explicit.

Directions: Respond to the following questions to model reasoning that first-grade students might exhibit in a higher-level-cognitive-demand mathematical task.

A full box of crayons has 18 crayons.

1. If there are 9 crayons in the first row in the box, how many crayons are in the second row of the box?

2. Six of the crayons are broken. How many crayons are not broken?

3. If you put the crayons in groups of two, how many groups of two will you have?

4. If you put the crayons in groups of three, how many groups of three will you have?

5. Can you make other groups with each group having the same number of crayons? If so, what are the groups?

6. Write the number name by counting each crayon by ones. Here is how you start.

   One

   Two

   Three

   Four

7. If you lost seven of the crayons, how many crayons would still be in the box?

Figure 2.14: First-grade higher-level-cognitive-demand mathematical task for reasoning.

Visit **go.solution-tree.com/mathematicsatwork** to download a reproducible version of this figure.

Directions: Consider the higher-level-cognitive-demand task involving crayons presented in figure 2.14 (page 95). Discuss with your collaborative team how a data-collection tool such as this one might support an effective formative assessment process.

Student Name	Working Task by Counting Proficiently With a Model (Box of Crayons, Countable Objects, and so on)	Working Task by Counting Proficiently Without a Model	Creating Drawings That Indicate Sense Making and Reasoning	Showing an Extension of Learning by Responding to Formative Feedback
Student 1				
Student 2				
Student 3				
Student 4				
Overall Observations of Student Work on the Task				

Figure 2:15: During-instruction formative assessment process tool.

Visit **go.solution-tree.com/mathematicsatwork** to download a reproducible version of this figure.

Planning for the Formative Assessment Process

You and your collaborative team can use the formative assessment process planning tools in this section—for grade K, grade 2, and grade 4 (figures 2.16, 2.17, and 2.18, pages 97, 98, and 99, respectively)—to plan for the formative assessment process. As you use higher-level-cognitive-demand mathematical tasks within the context of the Mathematical Practices (what students are to *do*), your plans for creating a formative assessment process in class can unfold. Keep in mind that the practices focus on student engagement with the tasks rather than teacher engagement. The key is how you choose to orchestrate and effectively provide feedback to students as they work on the mathematical task.

Directions: Consider the following higher-level-cognitive-demand mathematical task. Respond to each question to prepare for formative assessment.

Task for Grade K (K.CC.C.6)

There were 2 bowls of fruit on the table. One bowl held 9 bananas. The other bowl held 6 apples. Sam wanted to make his lunch with 1 banana and 1 apple every day. How many lunches can Sam make? Which bowl will still have fruit in it when Sam is done? How can a picture help you?

Which Mathematical Practice can students best develop proficiency in by working on this task?	What types of questions can you ask students to help guide their work on this task?	What can you learn about the mathematics that students know when they work on this task?	What can you learn about the mathematics that challenges students when they work on this task?
How do you plan to respond to student solutions and explanations?	**What changes will you make to the task the next time you use it in instruction?**	**What type of feedback prompts will support student learning of the content and related Mathematical Practices?**	**What questions might you ask to extend student thinking related to this task?**

Figure 2.16: Planning for the formative assessment process—grade K.

Visit **go.solution-tree.com/mathematicsatwork** to download a reproducible version of this figure.

Directions: Consider the following higher-level-cognitive-demand mathematical task. Respond to each question to prepare for formative assessment.

Task for Grade 2 (2.MD.C.8)

Last week, Tanji emptied her piggy bank and counted all of her coins, so she could take the money to the bank and deposit it. When she returned home, she noticed that she had accidentally left eight coins (the coins included three different values) on the floor. What is the greatest amount of money Tanji could have left on the floor? What is the least amount of money Tanji could have left on the floor?

Which Mathematical Practice can students best develop proficiency in by working on this task?	What types of questions can you ask students to help guide their work on this task?	What can you learn about the mathematics that students know when they work on this task?	What can you learn about the mathematics that challenges students when they work on this task?
How do you plan to respond to student solutions and explanations?	**What changes will you make to the task the next time you use it in instruction?**	**What type of feedback prompts will support student learning of the content and related Mathematical Practices?**	**What questions might you ask to extend student thinking related to this task?**

Figure 2.17: Planning for the formative assessment process—grade 2.

Visit **go.solution-tree.com/mathematicsatwork** to download a reproducible version of this figure.

Directions: Consider the following higher-level-cognitive-demand mathematical task. Respond to each question to prepare for formative assessment.

Task for Grade 4 (4.MD.A.3)

Kate wants to create rectangular designs for her new scrapbooking project. She has some card stock from which to cut designs. For some designs, she wants three rectangles with the same area but three different perimeters. For other designs, she wants three rectangles with three different areas but the same perimeter. Use grid paper to provide six examples to show how Kate might create all of these designs.

Which Mathematical Practice can students best develop proficiency in by working on this task?	What types of questions can you ask students to help guide their work on this task?	What can you learn about the mathematics that students know when they work on this task?	What can you learn about the mathematics that challenges students when they work on this task?
How do you plan to respond to student solutions and explanations?	**What changes will you make to the task the next time you use it in instruction?**	**What type of feedback prompts will support student learning of the content and related Mathematical Practices?**	**What questions might you ask to extend student thinking related to this task?**

Figure 2.18: Planning for the formative assessment process—grade 4.

Visit **go.solution-tree.com/mathematicsatwork** to download a reproducible version of this figure.

As you and your collaborative team discuss how to use planning tools to collect formative assessment data on each student or student team, consider how the tools in figures 2.16, 2.17, and 2.18 help you organize your data in ways that support easy use in the classroom. Revise the tools to best meet the needs that you and your team are identifying in the learning process for your students. Consider how the tools facilitate providing action steps for your students.

Do your students take more responsibility for their learning by reflecting on their work and viewing mistakes as learning opportunities? This is essential if student learning is to become formative in your classroom. As Dylan Wiliam (2007) indicates, in order to "improve the quality of learning within the system, to be formative, feedback needs to contain an implicit or explicit recipe for future action" (p. 1062).

Students then view assessment of their work as something they *do* in order to focus their energy and effort for future learning. A great place for this type of student reflection is during small-group discourse as your students work together on various problems or tasks and you walk around the room, check for understanding, and provide students with meaningful feedback, scaffolding, and advancing prompts that differentiate the task for them.

Thus, students and teachers share the responsibility of successfully implementing the in-class formative assessment practices. When your students can demonstrate understanding, they connect better to the actual learning standard for a unit and can reflect on their individual progress toward that learning standard. You support students' progress by using immediate and effective feedback during daily classroom conversations.

Connecting In-Class Formative Assessment Processes to the End-of-Unit Common Assessment

One outcome of effective formative assessment is that students will be prepared to showcase their learning on the common end-of-unit assessment you prepared before the unit. Recall the end-of-unit test in figure 1.21 (page 41) in chapter 1. It appears again here as figure 2.19.

The expectation is that before students engage in this common end-of-unit assessment, they have received timely and specific feedback from formative assessment opportunities. Through collaborative teamwork, you and your team members can benefit from the data you collect during the in-class formative assessment process. These actions should result in improved student performance on the end-of-unit assessment.

The common assessment in figure 2.19 provides insight into what was planned to happen during the unit of instruction. Use the end-of-unit assessment tool in figure 2.20 (page 102) to evaluate your team's progress, connecting your in-class formative assessment process to your end-of-unit assessment.

Now that you have considered how to support your students' development of mathematical understanding of both content and practices using formative assessment processes, you and your collaborative team should reflect on your progress.

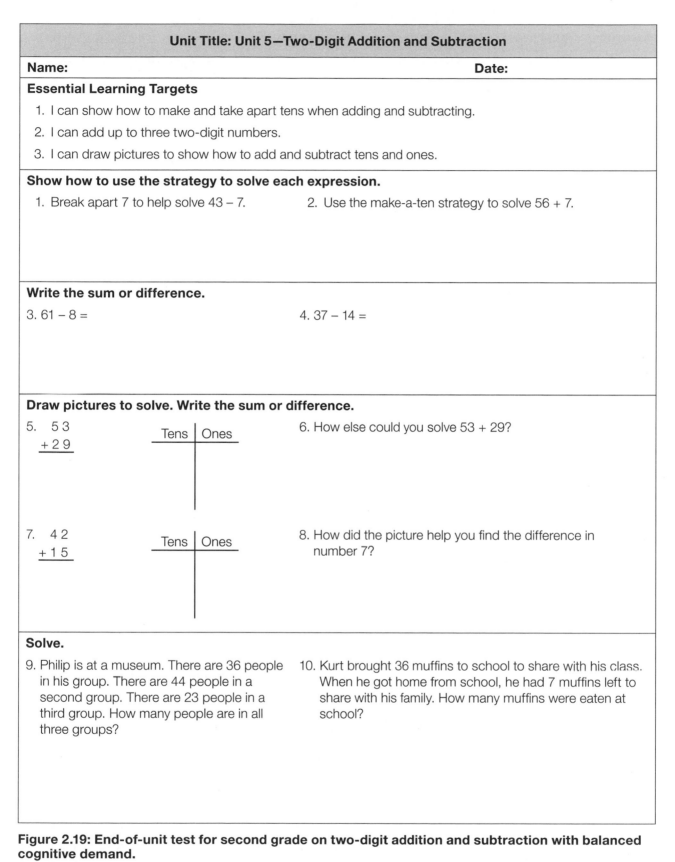

Unit Title: Unit 5—Two-Digit Addition and Subtraction

Name:	Date:

Essential Learning Targets

1. I can show how to make and take apart tens when adding and subtracting.

2. I can add up to three two-digit numbers.

3. I can draw pictures to show how to add and subtract tens and ones.

Show how to use the strategy to solve each expression.

1. Break apart 7 to help solve 43 − 7.

2. Use the make-a-ten strategy to solve 56 + 7.

Write the sum or difference.

3. 61 − 8 =

4. 37 − 14 =

Draw pictures to solve. Write the sum or difference.

5. 53
   +29

   Tens | Ones

6. How else could you solve 53 + 29?

7. 42
   +15

   Tens | Ones

8. How did the picture help you find the difference in number 7?

Solve.

9. Philip is at a museum. There are 36 people in his group. There are 44 people in a second group. There are 23 people in a third group. How many people are in all three groups?

10. Kurt brought 36 muffins to school to share with his class. When he got home from school, he had 7 muffins left to share with his family. How many muffins were eaten at school?

Figure 2.19: End-of-unit test for second grade on two-digit addition and subtraction with balanced cognitive demand.

Visit **go.solution-tree.com/mathematicsatwork** to download a reproducible version of this figure.

Directions: Select an upcoming common end-of-unit assessment. Discuss several actions taking place during instruction for the unit that will prepare students to be successful on the common assessment.

1. In what ways do you and your team members use a variety of formative assessment strategies to encourage students to make sense of what they were doing to solve mathematics problems?

2. How do students represent their learning in multiple ways—such as with numerals, drawings, tables, and charts?

3. In what ways do you and your team members demonstrate that the answer to a problem is not all that matters in learning; the reasoning and explaining process is also important?

4. In what ways do students improve proficiency with both concepts and procedures through experiences with higher- and lower-level-cognitive-demand mathematical tasks?

5. In what ways do you and your team members maintain the level of cognitive demand of higher-level-cognitive-demand mathematical tasks?

Figure 2.20: Preparing for the end-of-unit assessment tool.

Visit **go.solution-tree.com/mathematicsatwork** to download a reproducible version of this figure.

Formative Assessment and Your Tier 1 Differentiated Response to Learning

The recommendations of this high-leverage team action are linked closely to your Tier 1 RTI responses in class. These interventions are the core of an RTI model designed to support learning in class by every student. Douglas Fisher, Nancy Frey, and Carol Rothenberg (2010) suggest that "interventions are an element of good teaching" (p. 2) and these interventions begin in the classroom.

Tier 1 interventions are your first line of defense for struggling students and include your *differentiated* response to learning as you provide students and student teams with scaffolding prompts to help them think of other ways to solve a problem or higher-level-cognitive-demand task because you know they can explore a concept more deeply from a different point of view.

Within the RTI framework, differentiation is explicit and is purposefully planned by your team. You and your collaborative team can use formative assessment data, knowledge of students' prior knowledge, language, and diverse culture to offer students in the same class different teaching and learning opportunities to address student learning needs—especially as you give students feedback on their progress and they take action with their peers. By using formative assessment strategies, you are not making the content easier; you are making the content more accessible by the time the class period ends.

Your willingness and adaptability to try different teaching strategies and solution pathways to help all students understand the learning of the standard is in and of itself a Tier 1 intervention response. No matter how great the lesson, if it doesn't result in student demonstrations of understanding, then seeking other ways to teach the standard is a great Tier 1 teacher-led response. For more guidance on the nature of your Tier 1 response, see chapter 5 in our *Common Core Mathematics in a PLC at Work* series (Kanold, Larson, Fennell, Adams, Dixon, Kobett, & Wray, 2012a, 2012b).

Your Team's Progress

It is helpful to diagnose your team's current reality and action during the unit. Ask each team member to individually assess your team on the seventh high-leverage team action using the status check tool in table 2.4. Discuss your perception of your team's progress on using in-class formative assessment processes effectively. As your team seeks stage IV—sustaining—you will increase rigor, coherence, and fidelity toward student improvement and demonstration of proficiency in various Mathematical Practices and processes during the unit of instruction. You will also support deeper levels of student understanding for the learning standards, increasing students' chances for success on the end-of-unit assessment.

Table 2.4: During-the-Unit Status Check Tool for HLTA 7—Using In-Class Formative Assessment Processes Effectively

Directions: Discuss your perception of your team's progress on the seventh high-leverage team action—using in-class formative assessment processes effectively.

Stage I: Pre-Initiating	Stage II: Initiating	Stage III: Developing	Stage IV: Sustaining
We do not attend to or discuss formative assessment processes in our instruction.	We have discussed formative assessment processes and do not need to do so again.	We emphasize to students the value of using formative assessment feedback during class and taking action during class.	We always use in-class formative assessment processes to inform students' reasoning and learning.
We do not have a clear understanding of the difference between checking for understanding and formative assessment processes.	We discuss and use checking for understanding methods in class, but do not provide feedback or expect action.	We plan for student reasoning and sense making, and it is built into a formative feedback process in class.	We engage, as a team, in deep planning for formative assessment processes through the use of small-group discourse with teacher feedback and student action.
We do not know the in-class formative assessment methods used or expected by other members of our team.	We do not plan for how to engage students in formative assessment processes and practices as part of our team focus for each unit.	We plan for effective small-group student team activities as a way to promote the formative assessment process in class.	We discuss and implement well-developed formative assessment procedures to use with many of our higher-level-cognitive-demand tasks.
We do not use in-class formative feedback with student action in order to develop students' mathematical practice and learning.	We have not yet reached team agreement on how to use differentiated and targeted in-class Tier 1 RTI supports as part of our instruction.	We do not know the Tier 1 RTI response in class by other members of our team.	We discuss and use intentional differentiated and targeted in-class Tier 1 RTI supports as students engage in common higher-level-cognitive-demand mathematical tasks.

Visit **go.solution-tree.com/mathematicsatwork** to download a reproducible version of this table.

So much of student learning depends on the decisions you make every day. Will you use a robust set of mathematical tasks? Will you become intentional about using effective in-class formative assessment processes that exhibit meaningful feedback with subsequent student action? It is a lot to ask of your teaching every day.

To help you become more organized in how you might think through your daily mathematics instruction, this chapter concludes with the eighth high-leverage team action—using a lesson-design process for lesson planning and collective team inquiry.

You can ensure student learning of unit content standards and proficiency in Mathematical Practices and processes when your collaborative team has a good understanding of each Mathematical Practice, agrees on the meaning of *proficiency* for each Mathematical Practice, and uses effective formative assessment processes during instruction. All of these elements come together in this final section of chapter 2.

HLTA 8: Using a Lesson-Design Process for Lesson Planning and Collective Team Inquiry

Visible learning means an enhanced role for teachers, as they become evaluators of their own and each other's teaching.

—John Hattie

The eighth high-leverage team action highlights the team's work to develop and use daily mathematics lessons that encourage students to think deeply about the learning standards and to demonstrate proficiency in the Mathematical Practices. Planning several well-designed mathematics lessons during the unit brings together all of the elements of the seven high-leverage team actions and becomes part of your personal and ongoing team challenge as your teaching becomes more visible to one another.

The What

Recall there are four critical questions every collaborative team in a PLC asks and answers on a unit-by-unit, ongoing basis.

1. What do we want all students to know and be able to do? (The essential learning standards)

2. How will we know if they know it? (The assessment instruments and tasks teams use)

3. How will we respond if they don't know it? (Formative assessment processes for intervention)

4. How will we respond if they do know it? (Formative assessment processes for extension and enrichment)

High-leverage team action 8—using a lesson-design process for lesson planning and collective team inquiry—ensures your team reaches clarity on all four of the PLC critical questions within your mathematics lesson. The lesson-design process ensures all team members possess a strong understanding of the intent of the standard for the lesson, the purpose of the tasks to be used, and the expectation of student mastery of the standard.

High-Leverage Team Action	1. What do we want all students to know and be able to do?	2. How will we know if they know it?	3. How will we respond if they don't know it?	4. How will we respond if they do know it?
During-the-Unit Action				
HLTA 8. Using a lesson-design process for lesson planning and collective team inquiry	▢	▢	▢	▢

▢ = Fully addressed with high-leverage team action

Effective mathematics instruction rests, in part, on your careful planning, as well as on the careful planning of your team (Morris, Hiebert, & Spitzer, 2009). Your grade-level collaborative teams are uniquely structured to provide time and support needed to interpret the essential learning standards, embed the Mathematical Practices into daily lessons, and reflect together on the effectiveness of your lesson implementation.

In this eighth high-leverage team action, you can use the lesson-planning tool during unit instruction. This tool (see figure 2.21, pages 107–108), adapted from the *Common Core Mathematics in a PLC at Work* series, is a way to support the focus and design of your mathematics tasks. It can help you plan for formative assessment feedback questions and evidence *during* the mathematics lesson. Consider the following three questions.

1. How do we expect students will express their ideas, questions, insights, and difficulties?

2. Where and when will and should the most significant conversations take place (student to teacher, student to student, or teacher to student)?

3. How approachable and encouraging should we be as students explore? Do students use and value each other as reliable and valuable learning resources?

Your collaborative team is most likely using some type of lesson-planning format or tool. What separates the Mathematical Practices lesson-planning tool from most other lesson-planning models is its focus on developing students' proficiency with Mathematical Practices and daily learning objectives.

This lesson-planning tool also specifically asks you and your team to consider both student and teacher actions during lesson planning, which helps you see learning through students' eyes and helps students become their own teachers. Thus, learning becomes more visible to you, your colleagues, and your students. One particularly powerful collaborative tool is lesson study. Lesson study is very effective (Gersten, Taylor, Keys, Rolfhus, & Newman-Gonchar, 2014; Hiebert & Stigler, 2000) as a collaborative protocol with a high impact on teacher professional learning. Your team can also use the Mathematical Practices lesson-planning tool as you participate in collective inquiry during the unit. In addition, the tool emphasizes the importance of selecting and using higher-level-cognitive-demand tasks along with the more common lower-level-cognitive-demand tasks to support students' learning of mathematics.

Unit:	Date:	Lesson:

Essential learning standard: List the essential learning standard for the unit addressed by today's lesson.

Learning objective: As a result of class today, students will be able to . . .

Essential standard for Mathematical Practice: As a result of class today, students will be able to demonstrate greater proficiency in which standard for Mathematical Practice?

Formative assessment process: How will students be expected to demonstrate mastery of the learning objective during in-class checks for understanding, teacher feedback, and student action on that feedback?

Probing Questions for Differentiation on Mathematical Tasks	
Assessing Questions	**Advancing Questions**
(Create questions to scaffold instruction for students who are "stuck" during the lesson or the lesson tasks.)	(Create questions to further learning for students who are ready to advance beyond the learning standard.)

Tasks	What Will the Teacher Be Doing?	What Will the Students Be Doing?
(Tasks can vary from lesson to lesson.)	(How will the teacher present and then monitor student response to the task?)	(How will students be actively engaged in each part of the lesson?)
Beginning-of-Class Routines How does the warm-up activity connect to students' prior knowledge, or how is it based on analysis of homework?		

continued →

Task 1 How will the students be engaged in understanding the learning objective?		
Task 2 How will the task develop student sense making and reasoning?		
Task 3 How will the task require student conjectures and communication?		
Closure How will student questions and reflections be elicited in the summary of the lesson? How will students' understanding of the learning objective be determined?		

Source: Kanold, Kanold, and Larson, 2012, p. 53–54.

Figure 2.21: Mathematical Practices lesson-planning tool.

Visit **go.solution-tree.com/mathematicsatwork** to download a reproducible version of this figure.

The How

Your team's work during the unit of instruction involves engaging one another in discussions about individual lessons. These lessons are focused on specific essential questions for the daily learning objective. If your team has used the before-the-unit high-leverage team actions to plan the unit, then all elements needed to carry out the lesson are in place. Now the act of teaching and learning for the unit begins.

Understanding the Mathematical Practices Lesson-Planning Tool

At this point, there are some aspects of the Mathematical Practices lesson-planning tool that you and your collaborative team should contemplate to be successful. Consider the following frequently asked questions and responses regarding the Mathematical Practices lesson-planning tool.

Question: Is the Mathematical Practices lesson-planning tool appropriate for all mathematics content?

Answer: Yes. Each individual component of the tool is conducive to any mathematics content. In addition, during instruction for the unit, the structure this tool provides helps students come to know what to expect in a mathematics lesson and, hence, provides them some opportunity to note consistency and structure in *doing* the mathematics of the lesson.

Question: Will the Mathematical Practices lesson-planning tool work in a class of diverse learners?

Answer: Yes. When the Mathematical Practices lesson-planning tool asks, "What will the students be doing?" there is no focus on any particular characteristic of the student. In other words, the question addresses any student and every student—this includes consideration at the individual student level. So, the question is relative to your students and their characteristics. Other things, such as the structure of the classroom, also determine what students will be doing. For example, when students are working during the small-group instruction activities, what they are doing looks very different from students who are working individually or participating in discourse during whole-group instruction.

Question: We know the use of effective formative assessment strategies requires the collaborative team to make a commitment to plan an in-class common formative assessment process. Where do we see evidence of this process in the Mathematical Practices lesson-planning tool?

Answer: Every point of the lesson provides the opportunity for your assessment of student understanding and collection of information. For that data collection to become part of a formative assessment process for the student, every student must adjust and respond to his or her feedback and interaction with you or his or her peers during the lesson.

As such, every point of your lesson should provide a student with the opportunity to experience an effective formative assessment process. For example, the tool's "Assessing Questions" section provides an opportunity for teachers to help students scaffold their learning on a task or lesson to persevere and make progress during the lesson and the unit.

Question: Is the Mathematical Practices lesson-planning tool only compatible with a specific mathematics curriculum or textbook series?

Answer: No. The Mathematical Practices lesson-planning tool supports all mathematics instructional designs, so it is compatible with any mathematics curriculum or textbook series.

Use the questions from figure 2.22 to work with your collaborative team to study the lesson-planning tool.

Directions: Closely examine the Mathematical Practices lesson-planning tool. In your collaborative team, discuss how you can use the lesson-planning tool to help your current efforts to plan mathematics lessons for your grade level.

1. What are important factors to consider when planning lessons for an in-class formative assessment process?

2. How can you use the Mathematical Practices lesson-planning tool's assessing and advancing questions to facilitate small-group student-to-student discourse and differentiate learning around the higher-level-cognitive-demand mathematical tasks you use during the lesson?

3. How does the Mathematical Practices lesson-planning tool support the elements of your lesson—both the learning standards and the Mathematical Practices?

4. How will each mathematical task you choose for the lesson ensure students will be actively engaged in the mathematics?

5. Consider your start-of-lesson and end-of-lesson routines. How do these routines connect to the learning objectives of your lesson?

Figure 2.22: Learning about the Mathematical Practices lesson-planning tool.

Visit **go.solution-tree.com/mathematicsatwork** to download a reproducible version of this figure.

A productive way to use the Mathematical Practices lesson-planning tool effectively is for one or two collaborative team members to enter lesson ideas into the tool and present it to the team for discussion and feedback. Team members can then contribute ideas and suggestions to revise the plan. Consider the sample Mathematical Practices lesson-planning tool on third-grade plane geometry in figure 2.23 (pages 111–113).

Based on your responses to the questions in figure 2.22 and the sample third-grade lesson in figure 2.23, there are important details to consider regarding the CCSS Mathematical Practices lesson-planning tool. First, take a close look at the assessing questions section. These questions are particularly important for situations when students need intervention support with "just in time" prompts to continue in their pursuit of developing a strong understanding of the mathematics. These questions can serve as a tool for scaffolding student or student-team learning. They can serve as models for ways students might develop their own questions to promote action in their learning. These questions will help your students with perseverance and give them confidence to engage in productive struggle as a positive outcome of class.

Unit: Plane Geometry   Date: November 17, 2015   Lesson: Compare and Contrast Quadrilaterals

Essential Learning Standard

3.G.1: "Understand that shapes in different categories (e.g., rhombuses, rectangles, and others) may share attributes (e.g., having four sides), and that the shared attributes can define a larger category (e.g., quadrilaterals). Recognize rhombuses, rectangles, and squares as examples of quadrilaterals, and draw examples of quadrilaterals that do not belong to any of these subcategories" (NGA & CCSSO, 2010, p. 26).

As a result of class today, students will be able to compare and contrast the following quadrilaterals: rectangle, rhombus, square, and trapezoid. (Note: For this lesson, *rectangle* only addresses nonsquare rectangles. Squares as rectangles will be the focus of a subsequent lesson; however, if students approach this concept, then the lesson will accommodate this natural extension of the concept of rectangle.)

Formative Assessment

Students will be expected to demonstrate mastery of the learning standard during in-class checks for understanding by:

1. Identifying (by name) select quadrilaterals

2. Describing (orally, in writing, or by drawings) select quadrilaterals

3. Describing (orally, in writing, or by drawings) similarities between select quadrilaterals

4. Describing (orally, in writing, or by drawings) differences between select quadrilaterals

Probing Questions for Differentiation on Mathematical Tasks

Assessing Questions	Advancing Questions
1. What is a quadrilateral?	1. Which of the select quadrilaterals are parallelograms?
2. What are some characteristics of rectangles?	2. Which of the select quadrilaterals can be described as regular? Irregular?
3. What are some characteristics of rhombuses?	3. What is the definition of *rectangle*?
4. What are some characteristics of squares?	4. What is the definition of *square*?
5. What are some characteristics of trapezoids?	5. What is the relationship between squares and rectangles?
6. How are [insert shape] and [insert different shape] similar?	6. What is the relationship between squares and rhombuses?
7. How are [insert shape] and [insert different shape] different?	

Targeted Standard for Mathematical Practice

Mathematical Practice 3: "Construct viable arguments and critique the reasoning of others" (NGA & CCSSO, 2010, p. 6).

Figure 2.23: Sample Mathematical Practices lesson-planning tool for third-grade plane geometry.

continued →

Tasks	What Will the Teacher Be Doing?	What Will the Students Be Doing?
	The teacher will be observing, asking questions, responding to student questions, providing appropriate resources for students, and providing targeted support to students.	The students will be actively engaged in the lesson by collaborating in small groups, responding to teacher and peer questions and comments, asking questions, using the learning tools, and recording their work as instructed.
Beginning-of-Class Routines Prior to this lesson, students have explored various two-dimensional shapes on an individual basis. The expectation is that students are already familiar with the shapes and concrete representations of the shapes.	The teacher will distribute a set of plane shape manipulatives (consisting of about ten different shapes); some shapes should be one of each of the select quadrilaterals; the other shapes should not be quadrilaterals. The teacher will ask students to group the shapes in whatever way the students decide. After perhaps one or two iterations of this (or until students group the shapes with four sides and not four sides), the teacher will draw the students' attention to just the shapes with four sides and define them as quadrilaterals.	Students will work in their small groups to sort the shapes, discussing among themselves how to characterize the two groups and why a shape might belong to one group or another.
Task 1 Students will be engaged in making sense of the learning standard by providing information about their prior knowledge. If needed, the teacher will activate this prior knowledge as students discuss similarities and differences between the plane figures.	The teacher will distribute one of each select quadrilateral cut from construction paper, a large piece of paper, and tape to each small group. The teacher will instruct the students to fold the large piece of paper into fourths and to tape one quadrilateral in each section of the paper. The teacher will instruct students to write what they know about the shape in each section. The teacher will introduce that the learning objective is for students to use what they know about each shape to compare and contrast the shapes.	Students will arrange each shape as the teacher instructed and proceed to discuss (within the small group) what they know about the shape, including the name of each shape. Students might discuss characteristics of the shape as well as where they see representations of the shape in their environment.
Task 2 This task will develop student sense making and reasoning by requiring students to consider the responses of other students and to use this information to check their own understanding.	The teacher will ask each small group to share its results on one or more shapes with the whole class. The teacher will develop a master sheet and record the groups' information. The whole-class information will fuel comparing and contrasting of the quadrilaterals.	As students listen to what other students know about the shape, they will check where there are similarities to what they've written, add additional notes to what they've written, voice disagreement with what other students share, and provide justifications for their disagreements.

Task 3 This task will require student conjecture and communication by promoting mathematical discourse that provides opportunities for debate and consensus.	The teacher will call out two shapes and ask students to compare and contrast (naming similarities and differences)—picking combinations among rectangle, square, rhombus, and trapezoid.	Students will respond (orally, in writing, or by drawing) with the similarities and differences between a pair of quadrilaterals. Students will ask questions of their peers regarding suggestions about similarities and differences between the shapes.
Closure The teacher will use assessing and advancing questions in a summary of the lesson to elicit student questions and reflections. The teacher's assessment of students' interactions during instruction and students' mathematics journal entries will determine understanding of the learning standard.	The teacher will distribute the four shapes to each student. The teacher will ask what characteristic all of the shapes have in common. The teacher will review each student's mathematics journal as students proceed with the task.	The students will tape the shapes into their mathematics journals. Beside each shape, the student will write characteristics of the shape. At the bottom of the journal page, students will write four statements to compare and contrast any two select shapes.

Visit **go.solution-tree.com/mathematicsatwork** to download a reproducible version of this figure.

The tool's advancing questions are necessary for students or student teams who might recall prior knowledge beyond the scope of the lesson or who otherwise are able to develop understanding more quickly than other students or student teams. The enrichment the advancing questions provide raises the cognitive-demand level of the task but still keeps students within the mathematical standards for the lesson.

Notice that the collaborative team only identified one Mathematical Practice in the third-grade sample lesson (figure 2.23). Others might be present during instruction and appropriate for the tasks; however, choosing only one or possibly two Mathematical Practices for a lesson helps ensure that emphasis is on student engagement. This is a helpful point to keep in mind as you and your team consider Mathematical Practices while planning lessons.

Less is truly more in this case. For the sample lesson, teachers selected Mathematical Practice 3— "Construct viable arguments and critique the reasoning of others"—for emphasis. Opportunities for students to engage in Mathematical Practice 3 occur when students write about what they know regarding the selected plane figures and then share this information within their student team or with the whole class. In selecting appropriate mathematical tasks you and your collaborative team provide the foundation for the small-group mathematical discourse that will promote students' justifications about the plane figures and how they do or do not relate to each other. Students' justifications of their understandings and interpretations of the understandings of others are probable ways Mathematical Practice 3 comes into play during this lesson.

You should work as a collaborative team to use the Mathematical Practices lesson-planning tool together at least once per unit—if not more often. As you become confident in the high-leverage team actions both before and during the unit, it will become easier to design, reflect on, plan, and implement more lessons *together*.

Lesson Study: Using the CCSS Mathematical Practices Lesson-Planning Tool for Collective Inquiry

During lesson study, your grade-level team develops an expectation related to student learning for the lesson. You and your colleagues identify a challenging mathematical concept for students, such as comparing and contrasting quadrilaterals, and then design a lesson *together* to address the chosen daily learning objective within the essential learning standard. In the process of the lesson design, your team explores ideas about student learning as it relates to the chosen essential standard.

Recall the more informal model for promoting the idea of lesson study and a collective inquiry into your teaching practice—for one or two collaborative team members to enter lesson ideas into the Mathematical Practices lesson-planning tool and present it to the team for discussion and feedback. In this case, all team members subsequently contribute ideas to and suggestions for revision.

When possible, observe the lesson you design as one team member teaches it, debrief about your observations, make changes to the lesson design, and then reteach the lesson with a final debriefing of the second instructional episode. It may seem time intensive for every unit, but try to commit to some type of collective inquiry or lesson study together at least once or twice per semester.

Our experience with grade-level teacher teams is that lesson study will be one of the best work activities you can do together. The benefit of lesson study is the professional learning that results in deep, collaborative discussions about content, mathematics instruction, and student learning.

Remember, use a lesson-study lesson to develop your expectations for learning around the Mathematical Practices. Choose a content standard you know to be problematic for students. Then, use various resources to learn more about the content, connections to other mathematical concepts, and what research informs you about student learning of the topic. By the end of the lesson study, you and your team members will have gained content and pedagogical knowledge. You will have also raised the level of respect and trust among team members. The lessons you learn and solution pathways you discover are valuable for future lessons as well.

You can then use the observation tool in figure 2.24 (page 115) as a simple way to record data about what students are doing during the lesson that your team prepares and observes together. Remember that the intent of the lesson study, and collective inquiry as a team, is not so much to observe *the teacher* as it is to observe *the students* and determine if they actually learned the standard via the tasks you chose for them to do that day. As Hattie (2012) states in the title of his book, *Visible Learning for Teachers*, the goal as you work together becomes more and more transparent.

Collaborative Planning and Collaborative Reflection

Collaborative planning is not the end to your team's work on lesson design. An essential final step is collaboratively reflecting on the success of the lesson as implemented in your team members' classrooms. Also important is what you can learn from each lesson and from each other to inform both upcoming lessons in future units as well as the design of a similar lesson for future implementation. Consider the reflection prompts in figure 2.25 (page 116).

Date:	Course:
Lesson Learning Standard: _____	

Lesson Design Components	Observations of Student Actions
Assessment (formative, embedded, and summative)	
Questioning	
Mathematical Practice	
Beginning-of-Class Routine	
Activity or Task 1	
Activity or Task 2	
Activity or Task 3	
Closure	

Figure 2.24: Lesson study student data observation tool.

Visit **go.solution-tree.com/mathematicsatwork** to download a reproducible version of this figure.

Directions: With your collaborative team, answer the following prompts after implementing the lesson designed from the CCSS Mathematical Practices lesson-planning tool.

1. What level of student engagement with the lesson tasks did you observe? Describe how more direction, support, or scaffolding might have been provided if necessary.

2. Did students produce a variety of solutions or use a variety of strategies? If not, how might the structure of the tasks be redesigned to make them more open?

3. Describe any unexpected or novel solutions that would be worth remembering and incorporating into future classroom discourse.

4. What student misconceptions became evident during the lesson?

5. Which solutions were discussed and in what order? How did those choices support the classroom discourse? Upon reflection, might other choices have been more productive?

Figure 2.25: Reflection debriefing prompts to follow implementation of the CCSS Mathematical Practices lesson-planning tool.

Visit **go.solution-tree.com/mathematicsatwork** to download a reproducible version of this figure.

Add your lesson reflections, including sample student solutions, to each lesson plan for the unit and keep them on file. Using an electronically shared folder will make these lesson notes readily available for future lesson planning. While this approach falls short of formal lesson study, such reflection provides ongoing opportunities for you and your team to continuously improve each lesson and learn from your experience.

Creating a repository of collaborative lessons, including plans, mathematical tasks, sample student work, and reflections, is an essential team activity so each member continues to improve and refine his or her professional practice. Ultimately, this activity should increase the quality of your team's instruction and your students' learning. If you have not yet established such a repository, doing so is an important component of collaborative planning.

Your Team's Progress

It is helpful to diagnose your team's current reality and action during the unit. Ask each team member to individually assess your team on the eighth high-leverage team action using the status check tool in table 2.5. Discuss your perception of your team's progress on using a lesson-design process for lesson planning and collective team inquiry. The real value in collaborating occurs in your discussions after you have tried the lesson. As your team seeks stage IV—sustaining—you increase the probability that all lessons contain an appropriate balance of higher- and lower-level-cognitive-demand mathematical tasks and provide opportunities for all students to benefit from your formative assessment lesson planning.

Table 2.5: During-the-Unit Status Check Tool for HLTA 8—Using a Lesson-Design Process for Lesson Planning and Collective Team Inquiry

Directions: Discuss your perception of your team's progress on the eighth high-leverage team action—using a lesson-design process for lesson planning and collective team inquiry. Defend your reasoning.			
Stage I: Pre-Initiating	**Stage II: Initiating**	**Stage III: Developing**	**Stage IV: Sustaining**
We do not use a lesson planning tool.	We plan for instruction using the Mathematical Practices lesson-planning tool or other lesson templates independently.	We develop common lessons, either using the Mathematical Practices lesson-planning tool or other lesson templates but do not discuss the implementation.	We develop and implement common lessons at least once per unit, either using the Mathematical Practices lesson-planning tool or other lesson templates.
We do not know if our lessons provide for student demonstrations of understanding.	We discuss student demonstrations of understanding but do not have a common agreement on how to achieve them.	We collaboratively agree on how students should demonstrate understanding but we do not make instructional adjustments based on those agreements.	We ensure all lessons contain successful opportunities for students to demonstrate understanding.
We do not know about lesson study.	We have read about lesson study but do not create the time to do it.	We have engaged in a team lesson study but not as an ongoing practice.	We actively engage in a team lesson study once per unit and debrief in order to learn more about our students and to learn from each other.

Visit **go.solution-tree.com/mathematicsatwork** to download a reproducible version of this table.

Your team discussions about the daily lessons will ensure alignment to your unit learning standards and will allow your team to make adjustments to in-class practices and student actions during the unit.

Setting Your During-the-Unit Priorities for Team Action

When your school functions as a PLC, your grade-level collaborative team must make a commitment to reach agreement on the three high-leverage team actions outlined in this chapter.

> HLTA 6. Using higher-level-cognitive-demand mathematical tasks effectively
>
> HLTA 7. Using in-class formative assessment processes effectively
>
> HLTA 8. Using a lesson-design process for lesson planning and collective team inquiry

As a team, reflect together on the stages you identified with for each of the three team actions. Based on the results, what should be your team's priority? Use figure 2.26 to focus your time and energy on actions you deemed most urgent in your team's preparation and reflection during the unit. Remember, always plan lessons from the students' point of view. The following questions are at the heart of your during-the-unit work with your team: What will your students be doing during every aspect of the lesson? How will you provide formative feedback to them? How will they be expected to take action on that feedback? Focus on these few, but complex, tasks and work to integrate them into all of the planning and delivery of lessons for you and your team.

Remember the three high-leverage team actions in this chapter reflect steps two and three of the PLC teaching-assessing-learning cycle (see figure 2.1, page 68) and will help you prepare for the challenges of teaching and learning during the unit. They are also linked to teacher actions that will significantly impact student learning in your class.

Our attention now turns to chapter 3, and to steps four and five of the PLC teaching-assessing-learning cycle, with a focus on implementing a formative assessment process in response to the end-of-unit common assessments, your team's and your students' formative response to the data revealed at the end of the unit, and the impact on instruction during the next unit of study.

Directions: Identify (circle) the stage you rated your team for each of the three high-leverage team actions, and provide a brief rationale.

6. Using higher-level-cognitive-demand mathematical tasks effectively

   Stage I: Pre-Initiating   Stage II: Initiating   Stage III: Developing   Stage IV: Sustaining

   Reason: _____

   _____

   _____

   _____

   _____

   _____

7. Using in-class formative assessment processes effectively

   Stage I: Pre-Initiating   Stage II: Initiating   Stage III: Developing   Stage IV: Sustaining

   Reason: _____

   _____

   _____

   _____

   _____

   _____

8. Using a lesson-design process for lesson planning and collective team inquiry

   Stage I: Pre-Initiating   Stage II: Initiating   Stage III: Developing   Stage IV: Sustaining

   Reason: _____

   _____

   _____

   _____

   _____

   _____

With your collaborative team, respond to the red light, yellow light, and green light prompts for the high-leverage team actions that you and your team believe are most urgent.

Red light: Indicate one activity you will stop doing that limits effective implementation of each high-leverage team action.

Yellow light: Indicate one activity you will continue to do to be effective for each high-leverage team action.

Green light: Indicate one activity you will begin to do immediately to become more effective with each high-leverage team action.

Figure 2.26: Setting your collaborative team's during-the-unit priorities.

Visit **go.solution-tree.com/mathematicsatwork** to download a reproducible version of this figure.

CHAPTER 3

After the Unit

You can't learn without feedback. . . . It's not teaching that causes learning. It's the attempts by the learner to perform that cause learning, dependent upon the quality of the feedback and opportunities to use it. A single test of anything is, therefore, an incomplete assessment. We need to know whether the student can use the feedback from the results.

—Grant Wiggins

You have just taught the unit and given your common end-of-unit assessment. Did students reach the proficiency targets for the unit's essential learning standards? How do you know? How do your students know? More importantly, what are the responsibilities of your collaborative team after the unit ends?

Your after-the-unit-ends high-leverage team actions support steps four and five of the PLC teaching-assessing-learning cycle (see figure 3.1).

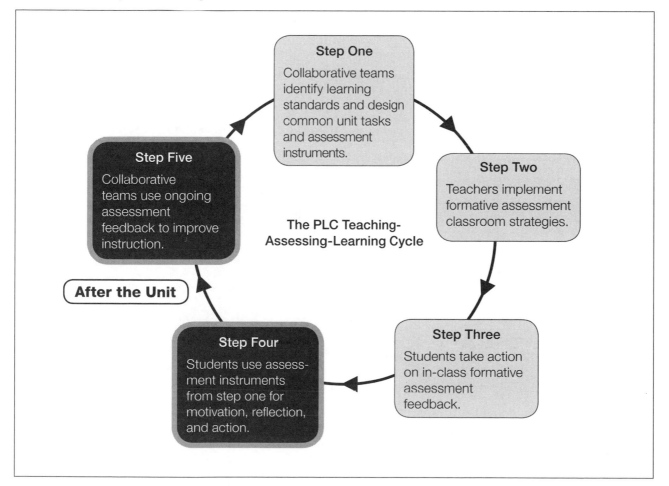

Source: Kanold, Kanold, & Larson, 2012.

Figure 3.1: Steps four and five of the PLC teaching-assessing-learning cycle.

Think about the last time you passed back an end-of-unit assessment. Did assigning the student a score or grade motivate the student to continue to learn and use the results as part of a formative assessment process? Did the process of learning the essential standards from the previous unit stop for the student as the next unit began? In a PLC, the answers are simple: the process of student growth and demonstrations of learning *never* stop.

Recall that in step one (chapter 1), your collaborative team unpacked the essential learning standards for the unit, identified meaningful mathematical tasks to balance cognitive demand, created the common assessment instruments for the unit with scoring rubrics, agreed to proficiency targets for the essential learning standards, and agreed to common homework assignments that support students' conceptual understanding and procedural fluency.

In steps two and three (chapter 2), the focus was on what students were doing in class—how your collaborative team developed and implemented lessons that encouraged students to demonstrate the Standards for Mathematical Practice and incorporated the effective use of formative assessment processes. You used the lesson-planning tool to organize the mathematical tasks you developed with chapter 1 into class-ready lessons.

Now, in step four of the PLC teaching-assessing-learning cycle, you investigate the process of consistent and accurate scoring of the common assessment instrument for immediate and constructive feedback to guide student learning. You examine the role your students play in using your feedback to set new proficiency targets and take action on their learning progress.

Finally, in step five, you will consider ways in which you work as part of your collaborative team—reflecting on student performance during the unit, adjusting your decisions about the next unit based on that information, and taking action as needed based on the end-of-unit assessment results.

To complete the analysis expected in steps four and five, you and your collaborative team engage in the final two high-leverage team actions.

> HLTA 9. Ensuring evidence-based student goal setting and action for the next unit of study
>
> HLTA 10. Ensuring evidence-based adult goal setting and action for the next unit of study

As Hattie (2012) states:

> My role as a teacher is to evaluate the effect I have on my students. . . . This requires that teachers gather defensible and dependable evidence from many sources, and hold collaborative discussions with colleagues and students about this evidence, thus making the effect of their teaching visible to themselves and to others. (p. 19)

The PLC teaching-assessing-learning cycle allows teacher and student reflection around evidence of learning on a unit-by-unit basis throughout the year and provides for a progression of learning beyond the end of the unit.

HLTA 9: Ensuring Evidence-Based Student Goal Setting and Action for the Next Unit of Study

Indeed, the whole purpose of feedback should be to increase the extent to which students become owners of their own learning.

—Dylan Wiliam

Continue your reflection on your last end-of-unit assessment. Learning should not stop when your collaborative team provides meaningful assessment feedback to students. Learning should be a required student action for reflection based on performance for each essential learning standard tested.

Wiliam (2007) makes the distinction between using assessment instruments for the three purposes of (1) monitoring, (2) diagnosing, or (3) formatively assessing. He states:

> An assessment monitors learning to the extent it provides information about whether the student, class or school is learning or not; it is diagnostic to the extent it provides information about what is going wrong, and it is formative to the extent it provides information about what to do about it. (p. 1062)

One way to characterize the type of assessment you are using is to examine how you and your collaborative team expect students to use the results. For example, diagnostic assessment of student performance is not sufficient for the student. A total score does not tell the student what he or she needs to do differently to learn the unit's essential standards, nor does it indicate the expectation that the student is to take any action on errors from the assessment.

Thus, a key formative assessment feature after the unit ends will be the process you have in place for your students to use and respond to the results of their assessment performance.

The What

Once again, recall there are four critical questions every collaborative team in a PLC asks and answers on an ongoing, unit-by-unit basis.

1. What do we want all students to know and be able to do? (The essential learning standards)

2. How will we know if they know it? (The assessment instruments and tasks teams use)

3. How will we respond if they don't know it? (Formative assessment processes for intervention)

4. How will we respond if they do know it? (Formative assessment processes for extension and enrichment)

High-leverage team action 9—ensuring evidence-based student goal setting and action for the next unit of study—guarantees your students use common end-of-unit assessment results as part of a formative assessment process that responds to critical questions three and four. What is the expected after-the-unit response if students demonstrate there are aspects of the essential learning standards they do or do not know?

In many classrooms, students typically receive their assessment back from their teacher, look at their score, become excited or sad (depending on the score), and place the paper in their notebook or backpack never to be seen again (unless it was a good score, which means it may end up on the refrigerator at home). This action of locking away the assessment wastes a valuable formative learning opportunity for your students.

Your team's work on this high-leverage team action will diminish that response. Your students will reflect on their successes and respond to evidence of weakness if the assessment instrument encourages formative student learning.

High-Leverage Team Action	1. What do we want all students to know and be able to do?	2. How will we know if they know it?	3. How will we respond if they don't know it?	4. How will we respond if they do know it?
After-the-Unit Action				
HLTA 9. Ensuring evidence-based student goal setting and action for the next unit of study			▨	▨

▨ = Fully addressed with high-leverage team action

In many elementary schools, support for students based on results of the formative assessment process typically lasts thirty minutes a day. This intervention work is on essential learning standards for students who have not yet achieved proficiency or who have met proficiency targets and are in need of enrichment work. All students should see assessment results as a means to better understand their current mathematical knowledge, to know their current levels of proficiency on the essential learning standards for the unit, and to be able to use the information on the assessment to improve their mathematical understanding during intervention. Assessment is an integral part of the learning process for students, which is why it is the link between teaching and learning in the PLC teaching-assessing-learning cycle and used from unit to unit.

The value of using assessment results includes two very important elements. First, students need to be given fair, accurate, specific, and timely (FAST) feedback on their work in order to improve their mathematical understanding. Second, students must have the tools and the opportunity to learn how to use their assessment results in formative ways as they set proficiency targets from unit to unit.

The How

As you and your collaborative team prepare to include students in the formative assessment process, you must provide students with feedback and ensure they take action. Using the tool in figure 3.2, make a list of the types of feedback you currently provide your students, and determine if that feedback requires students to take action or not. How could you revise the way students are expected to use the feedback so that it becomes actionable? Return to this list as you continue through this chapter.

Directions: Indicate the type of feedback you currently provide. Place a star next to the types of feedback with which students can take action. Note the action or revision students take based on the feedback.	
Type of Feedback You Currently Provide	**Student Action or Revision Based on the Feedback**

Figure 3.2: Formative feedback with action tool.

Visit **go.solution-tree.com/mathematicsatwork** to download a reproducible version of this figure.

To be part of a formative learning process for students, your feedback needs to require student action. However, it also needs to be meaningful and effective. Consider what the research indicates regarding what makes feedback effective.

Characteristics of Effective Feedback: FAST—Fair, Accurate, Specific, and Timely

Recall from your in-class formative assessment work with high-leverage team action seven (page 87) the essential characteristics of effective in-class feedback (Reeves, 2011). These same components of effective feedback hold true for your work with the end-of-unit assessments.

1. **Feedback should be fair:** Effective feedback on the test rests solely on the quality of the student's demonstrated work and not on other characteristics of the student.

2. **Feedback should be accurate:** Effective feedback on the test acknowledges what students are currently doing well and correctly identifies errors they are making. According to Stephen Chappuis and Rick Stiggins (2002), "Effective feedback describes why an answer is right or wrong in specific terms that students understand" (p. 42).

3. **Feedback should be specific:** Your test notes and feedback "should be about the particular qualities of [the student's] work, with advice on what he or she can do to improve, and should avoid comparison with other pupils" (Black & Wiliam, 2001, p. 6). Try to find the right balance between being specific enough that the student can quickly identify the error or logic in his or her reasoning but not so specific that you do the correction work for him or her. Does your test feedback help *students* correct their thinking as needed?

4. **Feedback should be timely:** Effective feedback on the end-of-unit assessment must be provided in time for students to take formative learning action on the results before too much of the next unit has taken place. As a general rule, you should pass back end-of-unit assessments and the results for proficiency to students within forty-eight hours of the assessment.

Consider the grade 3 task related to 6 × 7 presented in chapter 1 as a starting point as you and your collaborative team consider strategies for providing effective feedback.

Task for Grade 3 (3.OA.4)

A student in your class is asked to find 6 × 7 without drawing pictures. The student does not know the fact. Provide two different ways the student could use multiplication to find the fact by using other facts the student might know.

In chapter 1, we presented a sample web and conversation that included possible strategies students could develop to solve this mathematics task on property-based strategies to find 6 × 7 (see figure 1.3, page 12). Imagine that this task was included on an end-of-unit assessment. Figure 3.3 provides an example of student work.

I know that 6×7 means 6 groups of 7. If I know that 5 groups of 7 is 35, and then I have 1 more group of 7, I should add 35 and 7 to get 42.
Another way to get 6×7 is to know it is the same as 7+7+7+7+7+7, so I could skip count to get 7, 14, 21, 28, 35, 42.
So the answer is 42.

Figure 3.3: Sample student work for 6 × 7.

As an exercise in providing accurate and specific student feedback, you and your collaborative team should discuss the type of feedback you would give this student. Each team member should record his or her feedback to the student using the questions from figure 3.4 and then discuss.

Directions: Within your collaborative team, answer the following questions related to the student response to the 6 × 7 task.

1. How do the strategies the student used demonstrate his or her understanding of the learning standard the task assesses?

2. How does the feedback you generated build on the student's strengths to address the learning needs for the task?

3. How did the feedback you generated guide the student to understand an error (if you believe there was an error) without being too directive?

4. In what ways did the feedback you generated recognize student effort and accuracy?

5. In what ways did the feedback recognize the Mathematical Practices the student used for the task?

Figure 3.4: Student feedback discussion questions for 6 × 7.

Visit **go.solution-tree.com/mathematicsatwork** to download a reproducible version of this figure.

Your feedback should recognize that the student's response in figure 3.3 demonstrates that he or she understands the meaning of multiplication.

"I know that 6 × 7 means 6 groups of 7 things. If I know that 5 groups of 7 things is 35, and then I have 1 more group of 7, I should add 35 and 7 to get 42."

The first statement demonstrates that the student sees that multiplication represents the number of groups times the number of objects in each group. In addition, the student is able to use the distributive property (as discussed in chapter 1) to see that six groups could be viewed as five groups and one more group. Also, this response makes the connection to Mathematical Practice 7—"Look for and make use of structure." Student feedback to this portion of the response would highlight the student's strengths connected to the learning standard and practice for the task. However, the second part of the student's response, while also providing a correct product, does not demonstrate the same strengths.

"Another way to get 6 × 7 is to know it is the same as 7 + 7 + 7 + 7 + 7 + 7, so I could skip count to get 7, 14, 21, 28, 35, 42. So the answer is 42."

The second part of the student's response demonstrates that he or she understands multiplication as repeated addition and connects repeated addition to skip counting; however, unlike the first response, this response was not based on another fact as specified in the question. This is an example of where you and your collaborative team might have a conversation to determine an appropriate response. Is skip counting an acceptable strategy? Is it acceptable according to the directions? The responses to these questions are less important than the consensus of the team regarding the responses, whatever they might be.

As your team discusses each teacher's specific feedback, remember that improvement comes from acknowledging what students are currently doing well and guiding them to correct errors they are making. Effective feedback does not tell a student everything he or she needs to do, but rather it encourages the student to work to improve his or her knowledge and understanding.

You and your team can improve the quality of the feedback you provide by discussing your feedback in similar ways to the 6 × 7 example. It is important to make this a team discussion and not a private activity.

Use the student feedback team discussion tool in figure 3.5 (page 128) with an end-of-unit assessment. Pull a few examples of student work for each member to provide feedback. Share the feedback from each team member. Use the questions in figure 3.5 to consider how your feedback offers students opportunities to take action on their learning. What can your team do to continue progress with respect to the FAST feedback offered to students?

Be sure to also discuss the timeliness of your feedback to students. The use of fair, accurate, and specific feedback will not help students unless it is also *timely*. For example, if a student only provides one way to solve the problem, you can provide feedback hints on the assessment task that could guide the student to consider another approach, such as "What related facts do you know that could help you?" or "How could you use the doubling strategy?" However, if you provide this feedback to the student well after you give the assessment, your feedback will have minimal impact.

As a team, discuss your current practice for providing feedback to your students on the end-of-unit assessment. Is it timely and effective so students can take action?

Directions: Use your responses to these questions to guide the feedback you would offer students based on their responses on the assessment.

1. How do the strategies this student used demonstrate his or her understanding of the learning standard the task assesses?

2. How does the feedback you generated build on the student's strengths to address the learning needs for the tasks?

3. How did the feedback you generated guide the student to understand an error (if you believe there was an error) without being too directive?

4. In what ways did the feedback you generated recognize student effort and accuracy?

5. In what ways did the feedback recognize the Mathematical Practices the student used for the tasks?

Figure 3.5: Student feedback team discussion tool.

Visit **go.solution-tree.com/mathematicsatwork** to download a reproducible version of this figure.

Student Action on the Common End-of-Unit Assessment Feedback

When you return student work with your feedback on the end-of-unit assessment, your students need to be able to self-assess whether they are meeting the proficiency targets for each of the essential learning standards for the unit. Your feedback will allow students, with your support and perhaps schoolwide support, to engage in activities that lead to progress on the essential learning standards for that unit as well as for related standards within the grade.

Think of this expectation for student action as part of a Tier 2 response within the response to intervention (RTI) model discussed in chapter 2 (page xx). Tier 2 represents a targeted response to student learning and is part of your effort to answer the PLC critical question, How will we respond when students do not learn? For an in-depth discussion of RTI and Common Core mathematics, see chapter 5 from our *Common Core Mathematics in a PLC at Work* series (Kanold, Larson, Fennell, Adams, Dixon, Kobett, & Wray, 2012a, 2012b).

How can you and your team engage students in this feedback process for each unit? How can students become active partners in this formative end-of-unit process? Your team can build time during the instructional day to ensure the following four elements. Students:

1. Examine their end-of-unit results to determine whether or not they met the proficiency target for the unit's essential learning standards

2. Address errors on the assessment and use the assessment results to set goals and form a plan (either collaboratively between teacher and student or using a teacher-supplied plan)

3. Act on their plan during the next unit

4. Act on opportunities to improve their score on the end-of-unit assessment

You should work with your students to help them be responsible for their achievements and accomplishments in age-appropriate ways. This will look different for students in kindergarten versus students in fifth grade. Regardless of grade level, Tier 2 structures that allow your students to respond to the end-of-unit assessment feedback facilitate student goal setting (through proficiency targets) around the essential learning standards.

Figure 3.6, Student Action Plan Template for Response to an End-of-Unit Assessment (page 130), shows an action-plan model that you could use with students as you and your team prepare to return the results of an end-of-unit assessment. Notice the use of student-friendly language and sentence starters to encourage student participation at all grade levels. Please be aware that you will need to provide additional support for young learners and emerging readers.

Your team will also need to provide the structure and time of day so students can fulfill the actions they determine during the self-assessment. The best plan of action is to ensure that every day there is a period of time designated for this purpose—for providing extra time and support for the essential learning standards of the previous unit. Figure 3.7 (page 131) is a helpful tool for students to review their tests and self-assess.

Directions: How did you do? What do you need to do now? Think about this and answer these questions.

Student Name: **Teacher:**

Unit:

My Essential Learning Standards:

What were my learning standards for this unit?

"I can . . . _____."

"I can . . . _____."

"I can . . . _____."

My Learning Performance:

Am I getting closer to learning each standard? Did I meet the learning target?

"I can . . . _____."   Yes   No

"I can . . . _____."   Yes   No

"I can . . . _____."   Yes   No

For any learning standards you answered no:

I got _____ on this test. I will get _____ next time.

My Actions:

What will I do to get closer to my learning targets next time?

_____ Ask my teacher for help.

_____ Ask my partner for help.

_____ Ask for more time.

_____ Do more problems on my own.

_____ Get help online.

_____ Other actions: _____

_____

_____

_____

_____

_____

_____

_____

_____

_____

Figure 3.6: Student action plan template for response to an end-of-unit assessment.

Visit **go.solution-tree.com/mathematicsatwork** to download a reproducible version of this figure.

Directions: Review your test and complete the following.
Name:
Date: **Class:**

1. I did well on these standards . . .

2. What does the test tell me about what I do well?

3. I did not do well on these standards . . .

4. What does the test tell me about what I still need to learn?

5. Did all of my answers make sense?

6. Did I show all of my work and check my answers for each problem?

7. I am still confused about . . .

Which standards do I still need to learn?	**What will I do to learn them?**

What did I learn this time that I will apply to future mathematics tests?

Source: Adapted from Wallace, 2013.

Figure 3.7: Tool for student self-assessment and feedback.

Visit **go.solution-tree.com/mathematicsatwork** to download a reproducible version of this figure.

Any student who does not meet or exceed the proficiency targets for the previous unit must receive extra support from your collaborative team. This is a great opportunity for you to join forces with all team members and other school support personnel to provide intervention, extra practice on key tasks, and enrichment for those students meeting all essential learning standards.

Every student should be involved in some type of response to his or her performance from the previous unit. The results of the end-of-unit assessment should drive the intervention and support for your students and have an element of student goal setting as well (Kanold, Kanold, & Larson, 2012).

The intent of self-assessing student performance on the end-of-unit assessment is to help each student build responsibility for his or her own learning. While each student takes ownership for his or her individual progress on the learning standard, students may still work together to meet those standards. Student-to-student feedback is a vital component of the formative assessment process, and goal setting at the end of each unit is part of that student collaboration.

As you work with students to help them identify strengths, weaknesses, and the essential learning standards they still need to meet, what structures will you use to measure their progress? How will students work during the next unit to meet the learning standards they still do not know? They will need your help to take small steps toward reaching the learning standards from the previous unit. You may need to make a chart like the one in figure 3.8 for each student to record his or her current proficiency on each essential learning standard for future progress. You might choose designations, like levels, for students to achieve that have predetermined descriptions of understandings to be reached. For example, if students are working to apply properties of operations as strategies to multiply, a level one might be indicated by drawing groups of objects to multiply and level two might be doing skip counting, and so on. The key is that students understand the levels and can use them to determine personal progress. Alternatively, ask students to keep a journal or personal chart to record their own progress during the year.

My First Semester Standard Progress-Tracking Chart "I can . . ."											
Level 4											
Level 3											
Level 2											
Level 1											
Standards											

Figure 3.8: Student progress-tracking chart.

Visit **go.solution-tree.com/mathematicsatwork** to download a reproducible version of this figure.

For students with misconceptions identified through data on the end-of-unit assessment, your team could also develop a plan based on what works best for upcoming instruction. For example, if the next unit builds on the instruction from the current unit, tasks in the next unit should include small-group learning opportunities in which students can continue to work to address their misconceptions, developing proper prerequisite knowledge for the next unit. However, if the next unit contains new mathematical content standards, then the team needs to consider other options to support student learning.

This collaboration with peers and ownership of the learning pathway will engage students more deeply in the learning process and provide evidence for each student that effective effort is the route to mathematical understanding and success—an important lesson to learn early in life.

Your Team's Progress

It is helpful to diagnose your team's reality and action after launching the unit. Ask each team member to individually assess your team on the ninth high-leverage team action using the status check tool in table 3.1. Discuss your perception of your team's progress on ensuring evidence-based student goal setting and action for the next unit of study. It matters less which stage your team is at and more that you and your team members are committed to working together and understanding how to support students who still need help after the end-of-unit assessment as your team seeks stage IV—sustaining.

Table 3.1: After-the-Unit Status Check Tool for HLTA 9—Ensuring Evidence-Based Student Goal Setting and Action for the Next Unit of Study

Directions: Discuss your perception of your team's progress on the ninth high-leverage team action— ensuring evidence-based student goal setting and action for the next unit of study. Defend your reasoning.			
Stage I: Pre-Initiating	**Stage II: Initiating**	**Stage III: Developing**	**Stage IV: Sustaining**
We do not discuss whether our test feedback is fair, accurate, specific, or timely.	We discuss how our test feedback should be fair, accurate, specific, and timely, but we do not know what other team members actually do.	We provide fair, accurate, specific, and timely feedback to students but do not discuss its impact as a collaborative team.	We provide fair, accurate, specific, and timely feedback to students, and we discuss the impact of this feedback as a collaborative team.
We do not provide students with opportunities to respond to the feedback from the end-of-unit assessment.	We provide some constructive feedback to students on the end-of-unit assessment, but we do not require them to respond to the feedback.	We require students to correct their errors on the end-of-unit assessment.	We require students to correct their errors and identify the learning standards that are strengths and weaknesses.
We do not know the type of end-of-unit assessment feedback other team members use.	We do not have a team process in place for student response to the end-of-unit assessment results.	We work with each student to identify a plan for improvement and action based on end-of-unit results and improvement.	We work with each student to complete and carry out a plan for improvement and action based on end-of-unit results and improvement.

Visit **go.solution-tree.com/mathematicsatwork** to download a reproducible version of this table.

Your careful, honest, and open answers on the status check tool will allow for movement toward effective implementation of formative assessment strategies to assist students and teachers alike in the learning process. After reflecting on some of the work you and your team have done in chapters 1 and 2, you must now turn to the final high-leverage team action, HLTA 10: Ensuring evidence-based adult goal setting and action for the next unit of study.

HLTA 10: Ensuring Evidence-Based Adult Goal Setting and Action for the Next Unit of Study

> *[High-impact teaching] requires that teachers gather defensible and dependable evidence from many sources, and hold collaborative discussions with colleagues and students about this evidence, thus making the effect of their teaching visible to themselves and to others.*
>
> —John Hattie

The final high-leverage team action and second after-the-unit pursuit is to consider how your team uses the results of the end-of-unit assessment. While it is important for students to use feedback to monitor and improve their understanding of mathematics, it is just as important for your team to reflect on the unit assessment data.

The What

You and your team need to use the unit's assessment instrument result to monitor and evaluate your instruction. This provides a formative assessment learning process for your team, not just for the students. This high-leverage team action ensures your team reaches clarity on how to effectively respond *after* the unit assessment to the third and fourth PLC critical questions: How will we (as teachers and as a team) respond *after the unit ends* when students *do not* learn the essential learning standards for that unit? How will we respond *after the unit ends* when students *do* learn the essential learning standards for that unit?

High-Leverage Team Action	1. What do we want all students to know and be able to do?	2. How will we know if they know it?	3. How will we respond if they don't know it?	4. How will we respond if they do know it?
After-the-Unit Action				
HLTA 10. Ensuring evidence-based adult goal setting and action for the next unit of study			▩	▩

▩ = Fully addressed with high-leverage team action

Using the evidence from the common end-of-unit assessment, consider the following questions on your own and with your team.

- What went well in the unit?
- How well did students understand the essential learning standards of the unit?
- Which students need additional time and support to become proficient?
- Which students would benefit from an extension of the standard due to demonstrated proficiency?
- How well did we provide feedback to the students during the unit?
- How did the results vary by teacher? What are areas that warrant attention and need improvement for individual teachers as well as the team?
- How will we respond to the evidence of learning standards that did not result in student success?

The answers to these questions should not be based on personal reflection, but supported by the data from the common end-of-unit assessment. At this moment—step five in the PLC teaching-assessing-learning cycle (figure 3.1, page 121)—your team is charged with timely reflection on how your efforts during the unit did or did not meet with success. It is important to reflect before your team reaches too deeply into the next unit of instruction if the results are to have an impact on the instruction of the next unit.

Your collaborative team's unit assessment has its greatest payoff in this final high-leverage team action—using the student-performance results to make future instructional decisions for the next unit together. From a practical point of view, this sets up about ten cycles of planning and reflection for the year. This may seem too often at first, but with practice it becomes the norm in a PLC at Work culture.

Your team will need to focus on the messages contained only within the data and not allow other factors to influence your reflection. This is a key feature of the effective use of the common unit assessment instrument—how your team data reflect on student acquisition of the essential learning standards for the unit.

The process the students use to move their learning forward should be replicated for the adults on your team too. However, the learning relates to your plans and actions around interventions for students for the recently completed unit, your understanding of student performance from the completed unit, the learning for students to apply to the next unit, and the changes to make to the unit for the next year.

The How

Return to the most recent common end-of-unit assessment you and your team implemented. Consider the results of the end-of-unit assessment and what questions the data surfaced regarding the essential learning standards for the unit. Respond to the questions in the collaborative team data-analysis protocol in figure 3.9 (page 136) based on your objective review of the results. Your team's assessment has its greatest payoff in this final high-leverage action—ensuring evidence-based adult goal setting and action for the next unit of study.

Directions: With your collaborative team, answer the following end-of-unit assessment questions.

Team: _____

1. What went well overall in the unit?

2. What do the common end-of-unit data reveal about student performance on the learning standards with which students did well?

3. How did each teacher achieve these student successes?

4. What do the common end-of-unit data reveal about student performance on the learning standards in which students did *not* do well?

5. How well did we provide feedback to our students during the unit on the weak-performing learning standards during the unit?

6. What elements of the unit, including specific lessons, will need to be improved for future use?

7. What will be the impact on our instruction during the next unit based on our reflection on these results? (What will our RTI Tier 1 differentiated response be?)

8. How will our team provide for student re-engagement around learning standards that need more time and focus for student learning? (What will our RTI Tier 2 team response be?)

Figure 3.9: Collaborative team data-analysis protocol.

Visit **go.solution-tree.com/mathematicsatwork** to download a reproducible version of this figure.

In addition, make sure that the assessment results—how your students performed—are also free from scoring bias. One way to do this is to score your assessments together.

Collaboratively Scoring the Common Assessment Instrument

Consider the end-of-unit test from chapter 1 in figure 1.21 (page 41). Figure 3.10 shows a sample student response to tasks five and six along with the original scoring rubric.

Draw pictures to solve.

Write sum or difference.

5. 53
   +29
   ――
   82

Tens	Ones
||/||	XXXX
||	••••
	••••
	••••

6. How else could you solve 53 + 29?

\|\|\|\| (dot arrays)

Task	Scoring Rubric	Points	Task	Scoring Rubric	Points
5.	Represent 53 as 5 tens 3 ones.	1	6.	Represent solution to 53 + 29 correctly.	1
	Represent 29 as 2 tens 9 ones.	1		Use a strategy different from the one in number 5.	1
	Combine ones as 1 ten 2 ones.	1			
	Add to get 82. (Drawing supports Mathematical Practice 7.)	1			

Figure 3.10: Sample student work and scoring rubric.

Reflect on the three essential learning standards, the scoring rubric, and the proficiency targets established for this assessment before the unit began. How does the student work represent, or not represent, achieving the essential learning standards?

Figure 3.11 (page 138) provides useful questions for reflecting on the end-of-unit assessment data. You and your team should think about these questions as you examine the student work for questions five and six and how the questions relate to the essential learning standard "I can draw pictures to show how to add and subtract tens and ones."

For example, task five in figure 3.10 expects students to combine the ones in the two addends and make a ten. Specifically, students should be able to demonstrate that the three ones from the first addend and the nine ones from the second addend should be combined to make one ten and two ones. Next, students could demonstrate how that one ten would combine with the five tens and two tens from the two addends to create the sum of 82 as illustrated in figure 3.12 (page 139).

Directions: Answer the following questions to reflect on your student responses and work.

1. In what ways does the student work represent understanding of the essential learning standard?

2. What strategies did students use, and were they strategies that the team anticipated?

3. Could you follow the logic of the students' thinking or approach to each assessment item?

4. In what ways did the work depict any common student errors?

5. How does the student work represent proficiency with the Mathematical Practices?

6. Was the predicted level of cognitive demand appropriate for the assessment items?

7. Does this student work demonstrate what the team defines as successful for these assessment items? If not, why not?

Figure 3.11: Reflection questions on student work on an end-of-unit assessment.

Visit **go.solution-tree.com/mathematicsatwork** to download a reproducible version of this figure.

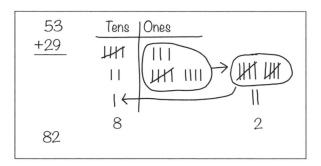

Figure 3.12: Sample assessment task strategy.

For assessment task six, there are many other strategies that students could use, including starting with the 53 and then decomposing the 29 into 7 + 22. This would allow the student to combine 53 and 7 to create 60, and then add in the balance of the decomposition (22) to create the sum of 82. This problem allows students to express their understanding of Mathematical Practice 7—"Look for and make use of structure"—as they consider the best ways to demonstrate their reasoning. Think about other strategies you discussed during your collaborative team's planning for the unit and your instruction as implemented during the unit. Consider how sample student work, such as figure 3.12, demonstrates your team's expectations for students and the level of success students experienced using specific strategies.

Scoring student work together will provide insight into other team members' mathematical thinking and allow you to consider the multiple ways that students and teachers represent their thinking. You can use the team activity in figure 3.13 (page 140) to facilitate a collaborative conversation.

Scoring common samples of student work also increases the likelihood of consistent scoring among team members. For common assessment data to have meaning during analysis, students should receive similar scores from any team member. This collaboration also provides opportunities for the team to have coherent and fair responses to whether or not each student met the proficiency targets set before the unit began.

These conversations could be helpful for your team collaborations concerning the proficiency targets that you need to set for the next unit. You will develop consistency through continued practice and open discussions about the reasoning behind each team member's scoring as your team looks to continuously improve at supporting students to achieve their learning standards.

Directions: Collect several student tests from your most recent common end-of-unit assessments.

Each member of your team should provide a low, middle, and high score, but do not label them. Make copies so that each member of the team has a complete set of student samples to score, removing student names, and number them for easy reference. Each member of the team should score the samples individually and take notes justifying the choice of each score. Next, the collaborative team should meet to share their scoring and notes.

Did everyone score the items the same? (If there are different scores on a sample item, discuss the reasons for scoring as a team.)

1. What are the reasons each team member has for the score they assigned that student?

2. What strategies did you use to agree as a team on a common score for each sample?

3. Organize your reflections on students' mathematical thinking in the following columns.

Student Name	Description of Student Work	Student Strengths	Student Misconceptions	Future Work With Students

Implications for instruction:

Figure 3.13: Collaborative team scoring and calibration activity.

Visit **go.solution-tree.com/mathematicsatwork** to download a reproducible version of this figure.

Setting Team Goals for Improvement

In order for you and your collaborative team to develop a cycle of continuous improvement, you need to set and reflect on collaborative team goals on a unit-by-unit basis. Consider the structure of clear and manageable goals using the SMART acronym through your team's lens (O'Neill & Conzemius, 2006).

- **Strategic and specific:** Our goals are aligned to essential learning standards.

- **Measureable:** We know when we achieve the essential learning standards.

- **Attainable:** We can achieve the goals through collaborative team efforts.

- **Results oriented:** We clearly define the outcome.

- **Time bound:** We have a specified time within which to achieve the goals.

Your team should set SMART goals (proficiency goals) for each of the unit's essential learning standards as you use the assessment results to prepare for the next unit. Your team can work on developing manageable short-term and long-term goals as well as orchestrating celebrations as students achieve the learning standards.

You create a SMART goal using your team's baseline data and use the goal as a framework to discuss current and future performance goals. Collaborative team SMART goals are always written and designed as "from" and "to" statements. As an example, consider the unit on two-digit addition and subtraction. A SMART goal for the unit might be: "We will increase student achievement on two-digit addition and subtraction *from* 67 percent meets or exceeds *to* 83 percent meets or exceeds based on the results of the unit four assessment by the end of November."

Additionally, imagine that your team's data at the end of November demonstrate that 83 percent of students met or exceeded proficiency on the assessment, and the team noticed that a high majority of those students used the same strategy. Does this success rate meet your SMART goal expectations for this learning standard? For the students who did not demonstrate proficiency, how will your team respond? Did your team expect that a majority of students would use the same strategy? How did the instruction you provided influence students' choice of strategy? These are the types of questions your team should reflect on when reviewing your SMART goals and common data with regard to the essential learning standards.

Use the reflection questions in figure 3.14 (page 142) to analyze your team's SMART goal performance from your common end-of-unit formative assessment and your team's plans for instruction moving forward.

Consider the third-grade essential learning standard, "Apply properties of operations as strategies to multiply and divide" (NGA & CCSSO, 2010, p. 23), explored in chapters 1 and 2 through the task based on finding strategies to multiply 6×7 using related facts. Our proficiency targets relative to the learning standard were for students to use strategies based on the commutative, associative, and distributive properties—did students use two or more of those properties in their work? Did an acceptable number of students meet that target?

Directions: Use these questions to reflect on your team's proficiency target performance and your future instructional plans.

1. Did the results of your team's data from your common end-of-unit assessment meet your proficiency target for each learning standard?

2. In what ways did the process of setting proficiency targets benefit your team's planning and implementation of the unit?

3. What are the proficiency targets your team needs to set for the essential learning standards in the next unit? Why?

Figure 3.14: Collaborative team proficiency target reflections.

Visit **go.solution-tree.com/mathematicsatwork** to download a reproducible version of this figure.

How did setting a proficiency target assist you in determining instructional strategies in your plan for the unit? In what ways were those plans actualized? How did you work with groups of students based on assessment data in your efforts to support students to use more than one strategy based on more than one property to multiply? How did this implementation technique using groups help you meet your proficiency target?

In what ways should the lessons we learned as a team during this unit of instruction influence our plans for proficiency targets for the next unit? Specifically, using the data regarding students' application of strategies to multiply, what is a reasonable goal for proficiency on our next unit focused on division?

In setting unit-by-unit student performance goals, your collaborative team needs to keep in mind that the focus should remain on the achievement of students—how can teachers help students grow in their mathematical understanding along all of the learning standards for the unit? Teachers should use student assessment data in considering the revision of both instructional and assessment practices within the collaborative team.

For further study and greater depth of knowledge regarding the SMART goal process, see the second editions of *Learning by Doing* (DuFour, DuFour, Eaker, & Many, 2010) and *The Handbook for SMART School Teams* (Conzemius & O'Neill, 2014).

Your Team's Progress

It is helpful to diagnose your team's current reality and action after launching the unit. Ask each team member to individually assess your team on the tenth high-leverage team action using the status check tool in table 3.2. Discuss your perception of your team's progress on ensuring evidence-based adult goal setting and action for the next unit of study.

Table 3.2: After-the-Unit Status Check Tool for HLTA 10—Ensuring Evidence-Based Adult Goal Setting and Action for the Next Unit of Study

Directions: Discuss your perception of your team's progress on the tenth high-leverage team action—ensuring evidence-based adult goal setting and action for the next unit of study. Defend your reasoning.			
Stage I: Pre-Initiating	**Stage II: Initiating**	**Stage III: Developing**	**Stage IV: Sustaining**
We do not set team proficiency targets for each essential learning standard.	We consider end-of-unit assessment results, but we do not set proficiency targets for each essential learning standard.	We independently use student end-of-unit assessment results to determine if proficiency targets were achieved.	We collaboratively use student end-of unit assessment results to determine if proficiency targets were achieved.
We do not know the end-of-unit results of other team members.	We provide some constructive feedback to each other at the end of a unit if asked.	We score some assessments together and calibrate for scoring accuracy.	We score all assessments together and calibrate for scoring accuracy.
We do not analyze end-of-unit results.	We analyze end-of-unit results but this does not influence our planning for the next unit.	We carefully and independently consider how end-of-unit results impact our planning for the next unit.	We collaboratively and carefully consider how end-of-unit results impact our team planning for the next unit.

Visit **go.solution-tree.com/mathematicsatwork** to download a reproducible version of this table.

After the unit ends, you and your team should have planned, implemented, and reflected on the instructional unit, the feedback you provided to students during the unit, the assessment instruments you designed to gauge student understanding, and both the student and adult SMART goals or proficiency targets set for that unit. This is a lot to focus on, so you will need to set your team's priorities.

Setting Your After-the-Unit Priorities for Team Action

As part of a PLC culture, your collaborative teamwork is never over, even after the unit ends. You have worked hard to pursue the two high-leverage team actions we outlined in this chapter.

> HLTA 9. Ensuring evidence-based student goal setting and action for the next unit of study
>
> HLTA 10. Ensuring evidence-based adult goal setting and action for the next unit of study

As a team, reflect together on the stage you identified for each of these team actions. Based on the results, what should be your team's priority? You can use figure 3.15 (page 144) to focus your time and energy on actions that are most urgent after the unit ends. Focus on these few, but complex, tasks and work to integrate them into your and your team members' practice at the end of each unit.

Directions: Identify the stage you rated your team for each of the two high-leverage team actions, and provide a brief rationale.

9. Ensuring evidence-based student goal setting and action for the next unit of study

    Stage I: Pre-Initiating   Stage II: Initiating   Stage III: Developing   Stage IV: Sustaining

    Reason: _____

10. Ensuring evidence-based adult goal setting and action for the next unit of study

    Stage I: Pre-Initiating   Stage II: Initiating   Stage III: Developing   Stage IV: Sustaining

    Reason: _____

With your collaborative team, respond to the red light, yellow light, and green light prompts for the high-leverage team actions that you and your team believe are most urgent to focus on.

Red light: Indicate one activity you will stop doing that limits effective implementation of the high-leverage team actions.

Yellow light: Indicate one activity you will continue to do to be effective with the high-leverage team actions.

Green light: Indicate one activity you will begin to do immediately to become more effective with the high-leverage team actions.

Figure 3.15: Setting your collaborative team's after-the-unit priorities.

Visit **go.solution-tree.com/mathematicsatwork** to download a reproducible version of this figure.

Your after-the-unit work consisted of (1) ensuring that each student receives effective feedback that is fair, accurate, specific, and timely and that students use the common assessment as a formative learning opportunity; and (2) ensuring consistent scoring for the common assessment instrument while ensuring students and adults use the common assessment results to identify achievement of proficiency targets and actions for the next unit of study and beyond. These pursuits address steps four and five of the PLC teaching-assessing-learning cycle (see figure 3.1, page 121).

The effective implementation of step five (your collaborative team using ongoing assessment feedback to improve instruction) leads you to cycle back to step one and begin the process again with the next unit, setting new short-term goals and shifting focus to the next unit of instruction. The cycle is a continuous-improvement process necessary for effective mathematics teaching, assessing, and learning.

What is wonderful about the process of teaching and learning is that both students and teachers improve their understanding of mathematical content, Mathematical Practices, and their role in the formative assessment process.

This chapter completes your investigation of the PLC teaching-assessing-learning cycle and the ten high-leverage team actions that deliver on the promise of improved student achievement.

EPILOGUE

Taking Your Next Steps

So now what? You and your collaborative team have moved through the stages of the PLC teaching-assessing-learning cycle, and should now be ready to start the process again with the next unit. Some of the considerations from this handbook relative to work with your instructional unit include:

> • Was the size of the unit manageable within the teaching-assessing-learning cycle?
>
> • How did your team discussion of essential learning standards help you to support student understanding?
>
> • How did the design of the mathematical tasks and assessment instruments work? Were they aligned?
>
> • How did the unit formative assessment plan fit with the end-of-unit assessment?

Figure E.1 (pages 146–147) provides a final summative evaluation your team can use at the beginning or the end of the school year to identify your current progress on each of the high-leverage team actions. Celebrate your strengths and prioritize your areas for continued growth.

Reflect on where your team falls along the continua for each high-leverage team action. The process of collaboration capitalizes on the fact that you come together to use diverse experiences and knowledge to create a whole that is larger than the sum of the parts. Your effective collaboration around these actions is *the* solution to sustained professional learning—an ongoing and never-ending process of teacher growth necessary to meet the expectations of the Common Core, and beyond.

The National Board for Professional Teaching Standards (2010) mathematics standards state it like this:

> Seeing themselves as partners with other teachers, they are dedicated to improving the profession. They care about the quality of teaching in their schools, and, to this end, their collaboration with colleagues is continuous and explicit. They recognize that collaborating in a professional learning community contributes to their own professional growth, as well as to the growth of their peers, for the benefit of student learning. Teachers promote the ideal that working collaboratively increases knowledge, reflection, and quality of practice and benefits the instructional program. (p. 75)

The new paradigm for the professional development of mathematics teachers requires an understanding that the knowledge capacity of every teacher matters. More importantly, however, is that every teacher *acts* on that knowledge and transfers the professional development that he or she receives into his or her daily classroom practice.

Assessing Your High-Leverage Team Actions

Directions: Rate your team on a scale of 1 (low) to 6 (high) for your current implementation of each of the ten high-leverage team actions.

Before the Unit (Step 1 of the Cycle)

HLTA 1. We agree on the expectations and intent of the common essential learning standards and Mathematical Practices for the unit.

Rating: _____

Reason: _____

_____

HLTA 2. We identify and discuss student use of higher-level-cognitive-demand mathematical tasks as part of the instruction during the unit.

Rating: _____

Reason: _____

_____

HLTA 3. We develop high-quality common assessment instruments for the unit.

Rating: _____

Reason: _____

_____

HLTA 4. We develop accurate scoring rubrics and proficiency expectations for the common assessment instruments.

Rating: _____

Reason: _____

_____

HLTA 5. We plan and use common homework assignments.

Rating: _____

Reason: _____

_____

During the Unit (Steps 2 and 3 of the Cycle)

HLTA 6. We develop student proficiency in each Mathematical Practice through in-class, higher-level cognitive-demand mathematical tasks.

Rating: _____

Reason: _____

_____

HLTA 7. We use in-class formative assessment processes effectively.

Rating: _____

Reason: _____

_____

HLTA 8. We use a lesson-design process for lesson planning and collective team inquiry.

Rating: _____

Reason: _____

_____

After the Unit (Steps 4 and 5 of the Cycle)

HLTA 9. We ensure evidence-based student goal setting and action for the next unit of study.
Rating: _____

Reason: _____

_____

HLTA 10. We ensure evidence-based adult goal setting and action for the next unit of study.
Rating: _____

Reason: _____

_____

Setting Your Collaborative Team Monitoring Priorities

Directions: Review your ratings for the ten high-leverage team actions under the three categories of essential PLC team commitments.

For each category, list your top two or three specific areas for improvement. Based on your knowledge of the team, what should be your focus for adult growth and improvement and knowledge capacity building? Be specific and use your ratings to inform your choices. Also examine your current progress on team-level SMART goals.

1. PLC Teacher Team Agreements for Teaching and Learning Before the Unit Begins

2. PLC Teacher Team Agreements for Teaching and Learning During the Unit

3. PLC Teacher Team Agreements for Teaching and Learning After the Unit Ends

4. PLC Teacher Team Agreements for SMART Goals

What data targets beckon for improved student achievement in each course or grade level for next year? Consider local (unit by unit), state (CCSS mathematics or otherwise), and national data-improvement targets.

Figure E.1: Tool for assessing your actions and setting your team priorities.

Visit **go.solution-tree.com/mathematicsatwork** to download a reproducible version of this figure.

APPENDIX A

Standards for Mathematical Practice

Source: NGA & CCSSO, 2010, pp. 6–8. © Copyright 2010. National Governors Association Center for Best Practices and Council of Chief State School Officers. All rights reserved. Used with permission.

The Standards for Mathematical Practice describe varieties of expertise that mathematics educators at all levels should seek to develop in their students. These practices rest on important "processes and proficiencies" with longstanding importance in mathematics education. The first of these are the NCTM process standards of problem solving, reasoning and proof, communication, representation, and connections. The second are the strands of mathematical proficiency specified in the National Research Council's report *Adding It Up:* adaptive reasoning, strategic competence, conceptual understanding (comprehension of mathematical concepts, operations and relations), procedural fluency (skill in carrying out procedures flexibly, accurately, efficiently and appropriately), and productive disposition (habitual inclination to see mathematics as sensible, useful, and worthwhile, coupled with a belief in diligence and one's own efficacy).

1. **Make sense of problems and persevere in solving them.** Mathematically proficient students start by explaining to themselves the meaning of a problem and looking for entry points to its solution. They analyze givens, constraints, relationships, and goals. They make conjectures about the form and meaning of the solution and plan a solution pathway rather than simply jumping into a solution attempt. They consider analogous problems, and try special cases and simpler forms of the original problem in order to gain insight into its solution. They monitor and evaluate their progress and change course if necessary. Older students might, depending on the context of the problem, transform algebraic expressions or change the viewing window on their graphing calculator to get the information they need. Mathematically proficient students can explain correspondences between equations, verbal descriptions, tables, and graphs or draw diagrams of important features and relationships, graph data, and search for regularity or trends. Younger students might rely on using concrete objects or pictures to help conceptualize and solve a problem. Mathematically proficient students check their answers to problems using a different method, and they continually ask themselves, "Does this make sense?" They can understand the approaches of others to solving complex problems and identify correspondences between different approaches.

2. **Reason abstractly and quantitatively.** Mathematically proficient students make sense of quantities and their relationships in problem situations. They bring two complementary abilities to bear on problems involving quantitative relationships: the ability to decontextualize—to abstract a given situation and represent it symbolically and manipulate the representing symbols as if they have a life of their own, without necessarily attending to their referents—and the ability to contextualize, to pause as needed during the manipulation process in order to probe into the referents for the symbols involved. Quantitative reasoning entails habits of creating a coherent representation of the problem at hand; considering the units involved; attending to the meaning of quantities, not just how to compute them; and knowing and flexibly using different properties of operations and objects.

3. Construct viable arguments and critique the reasoning of others. Mathematically proficient students understand and use stated assumptions, definitions, and previously established results in constructing arguments. They make conjectures and build a logical progression of statements to explore the truth of their conjectures. They are able to analyze situations by breaking them into cases, and can recognize and use counterexamples. They justify their conclusions, communicate them to others, and respond to the arguments of others. They reason inductively about data, making plausible arguments that take into account the context from which the data arose. Mathematically proficient students are also able to compare the effectiveness of two plausible arguments, distinguish correct logic or reasoning from that which is flawed, and—if there is a flaw in an argument—explain what it is. Elementary students can construct arguments using concrete referents such as objects, drawings, diagrams, and actions. Such arguments can make sense and be correct, even though they are not generalized or made formal until later grades. Later, students learn to determine domains to which an argument applies. Students at all grades can listen or read the arguments of others, decide whether they make sense, and ask useful questions to clarify or improve the arguments.

4. Model with mathematics. Mathematically proficient students can apply the mathematics they know to solve problems arising in everyday life, society, and the workplace. In early grades, this might be as simple as writing an addition equation to describe a situation. In middle grades, a student might apply proportional reasoning to plan a school event or analyze a problem in the community. By high school, a student might use geometry to solve a design problem or use a function to describe how one quantity of interest depends on another. Mathematically proficient students who can apply what they know are comfortable making assumptions and approximations to simplify a complicated situation, realizing that these may need revision later. They are able to identify important quantities in a practical situation and map their relationships using such tools as diagrams, two-way tables, graphs, flowcharts and formulas. They can analyze those relationships mathematically to draw conclusions. They routinely interpret their mathematical results in the context of the situation and reflect on whether the results make sense, possibly improving the model if it has not served its purpose.

5. Use appropriate tools strategically. Mathematically proficient students consider the available tools when solving a mathematical problem. These tools might include pencil and paper, concrete models, a ruler, a protractor, a calculator, a spreadsheet, a computer algebra system, a statistical package, or dynamic geometry software. Proficient students are sufficiently familiar with tools appropriate for their grade or course to make sound decisions about when each of these tools might be helpful, recognizing both the insight to be gained and their limitations. For example, mathematically proficient high school students analyze graphs of functions and solutions generated using a graphing calculator. They detect possible errors by strategically using estimation and other mathematical knowledge. When making mathematical models, they know that technology can enable them to visualize the results of varying assumptions, explore consequences, and compare predictions with data. Mathematically proficient students at various grade levels are able to identify relevant external mathematical resources, such as digital content located on a website, and use them to pose or solve problems. They are able to use technological tools to explore and deepen their understanding of concepts.

6. Attend to precision. Mathematically proficient students try to communicate precisely to others. They try to use clear definitions in discussion with others and in their own reasoning. They state the meaning of the symbols they choose, including using the equal sign consistently and appropriately. They are careful about specifying units of measure, and labeling axes to clarify the correspondence with quantities in a problem. They calculate accurately and efficiently, and express numerical answers with a degree of precision appropriate for the problem context. In the elementary grades, students give carefully formulated explanations to each other. By the time they reach high school they have learned to examine claims and make explicit use of definitions.

7. **Look for and make use of structure.** Mathematically proficient students look closely to discern a pattern or structure. Young students, for example, might notice that three and seven more is the same amount as seven and three more, or they may sort a collection of shapes according to how many sides the shapes have. Later, students will see 7×8 equals the well remembered $7 \times 5 + 7 \times 3$, in preparation for learning about the distributive property. In the expression $x^2 + 9x + 14$, older students can see the 14 as 2×7 and the 9 as $2 + 7$. They recognize the significance of an existing line in a geometric figure and can use the strategy of drawing an auxiliary line for solving problems. They also can step back for an overview and shift perspective. They can see complicated things, such as some algebraic expressions, as single objects or as being composed of several objects. For example, they can see $5 - 3(x - y)^2$ as 5 minus a positive number times a square and use that to realize that its value cannot be more than 5 for any real numbers x and y.

8. **Look for and express regularity in repeated reasoning.** Mathematically proficient students notice if calculations are repeated, and look both for general methods and for shortcuts. Upper elementary students might notice when dividing 25 by 11 that they are repeating the same calculations over and over again, and conclude they have a repeating decimal. By paying attention to the calculation of slope as they repeatedly check whether points are on the line through $(1, 2)$ with slope 3, middle school students might abstract the equation $(y - 2)/(x - 1) = 3$. Noticing the regularity in the way terms cancel when expanding $(x - 1)(x + 1)$, $(x - 1)(x^2 + x + 1)$, and $(x - 1)(x^3 + x^2 + x + 1)$ might lead them to the general formula for the sum of a geometric series. As they work to solve a problem, mathematically proficient students maintain oversight of the process, while attending to the details. They continually evaluate the reasonableness of their intermediate results.

Connecting the Standards for Mathematical Practice to the Standards for Mathematical Content

The Standards for Mathematical Practice describe ways in which developing student practitioners of the discipline of mathematics increasingly ought to engage with the subject matter as they grow in mathematical maturity and expertise throughout the elementary, middle and high school years. Designers of curricula, assessments, and professional development should all attend to the need to connect the mathematical practices to mathematical content in mathematics instruction.

The Standards for Mathematical Content are a balanced combination of procedure and understanding. Expectations that begin with the word "understand" are often especially good opportunities to connect the practices to the content. Students who lack understanding of a topic may rely on procedures too heavily. Without a flexible base from which to work, they may be less likely to consider analogous problems, represent problems coherently, justify conclusions, apply the mathematics to practical situations, use technology mindfully to work with the mathematics, explain the mathematics accurately to other students, step back for an overview, or deviate from a known procedure to find a shortcut. In short, a lack of understanding effectively prevents a student from engaging in the mathematical practices.

In this respect, those content standards which set an expectation of understanding are potential "points of intersection" between the Standards for Mathematical Content and the Standards for Mathematical Practice. These points of intersection are intended to be weighted toward central and generative concepts in the school mathematics curriculum that most merit the time, resources, innovative energies, and focus necessary to qualitatively improve the curriculum, instruction, assessment, professional development, and student achievement in mathematics.

Cognitive-Demand-Level Task-Analysis Guide

Source: Smith & Stein, 1998. Copyright 1998, National Council of Teachers of Mathematics. Used with permission.

Table B.1: Cognitive-Demand Levels of Mathematical Tasks

Lower-Level Cognitive Demand	Higher-Level Cognitive Demand
Memorization Tasks • These tasks involve reproducing previously learned facts, rules, formulae, or definitions to memory. • They cannot be solved using procedures because a procedure does not exist or because the time frame in which the task is being completed is too short to use the procedure. • They are not ambiguous; such tasks involve exact reproduction of previously seen material and what is to be reproduced is clearly and directly stated. • They have no connection to the concepts or meaning that underlie the facts, rules, formulae, or definitions being learned or reproduced.	**Procedures With Connections Tasks** • These procedures focus students' attention on the use of procedures for the purpose of developing deeper levels of understanding of mathematical concepts and ideas. • They suggest pathways to follow (explicitly or implicitly) that are broad general procedures that have close connections to underlying conceptual ideas as opposed to narrow algorithms that are opaque with respect to underlying concepts. • They usually are represented in multiple ways (for example, visual diagrams, manipulatives, symbols, or problem situations). They require some degree of cognitive effort. Although general procedures may be followed, they cannot be followed mindlessly. Students need to engage with the conceptual ideas that underlie the procedures in order to successfully complete the task and develop understanding.
Procedures Without Connections Tasks • These procedures are algorithmic. Use of the procedure is either specifically called for, or its use is evident based on prior instruction, experience, or placement of the task. • They require limited cognitive demand for successful completion. There is little ambiguity about what needs to be done and how to do it. • They have no connection to the concepts or meaning that underlie the procedure being used. • They are focused on producing correct answers rather than developing mathematical understanding. • They require no explanations or have explanations that focus solely on describing the procedure used.	**Doing Mathematics Tasks** • Doing mathematics tasks requires complex and no algorithmic thinking (for example, the task, instructions, or examples do not explicitly suggest a predictable, well-rehearsed approach or pathway). • It requires students to explore and understand the nature of mathematical concepts, processes, or relationships. • It demands self-monitoring or self-regulation of one's own cognitive processes. • It requires students to access relevant knowledge and experiences and make appropriate use of them in working through the task. • It requires students to analyze the task and actively examine task constraints that may limit possible solution strategies and solutions. • It requires considerable cognitive effort and may involve some level of anxiety for the student due to the unpredictable nature of the required solution process.

Sources for Higher-Level-Cognitive-Demand Tasks

Common Core Conversation

www.commoncoreconversation.com/math-resources.html

Common Core Conversation is a collection of more than fifty free website resources for the Common Core State Standards in mathematics and ELA.

EngageNY Mathematics

www.engageny.org/mathematics

The site features curriculum modules from the state of New York that include sample assessment tasks, deep resources, and exemplars for grades preK–12.

Howard County Public School System Secondary Mathematics Common Core

https://secondarymathcommoncore.wikispaces.hcpss.org

This site is a sample wiki for a district K–12 mathematics curriculum.

Illustrative Mathematics

www.illustrativemathematics.org

The main goal of this project is to provide guidance to states, assessment consortia, testing companies, and curriculum developers by illustrating the range and types of mathematical work that students will experience upon implementation of the Common Core State Standards for mathematics.

Inside Mathematics

www.insidemathematics.org/index.php/common-core-standards

This site provides classroom videos and lesson examples to illustrate the Mathematical Practices.

Mathematics Assessment Project

http://map.mathshell.org/materials/index.php

The Mathematics Assessment Project (MAP) aims to bring to life the Common Core State Standards in a way that will help teachers and their students turn their aspirations for achieving them into classroom realities. MAP is a collaboration between the University of California at Berkeley; the Shell Centre team at the University of Nottingham; and the Silicon Valley Mathematics Initiative (MARS).

National Council of Supervisors of Mathematics

www.mathedleadership.org/ccss/itp/index.html

This site features collections of K–12 mathematical tasks for illustrating the Standards for Mathematical Practice. The website includes best-selling books, numerous journal articles, and insights into the teaching and learning of mathematics.

National Council of Teachers of Mathematics Illuminations

http://illuminations.nctm.org

This site provides standards-based resources that improve the teaching and learning of mathematics for all students. The materials illuminate the vision for school mathematics set forth in NCTM's *Principles and Standards for School Mathematics*, *Curriculum Focal Points for Prekindergarten Through Grade 8 Mathematics*, and *Focus in High School Mathematics: Reasoning and Sense Making*.

National Science Digital Library

http://nsdl.org/commcore/math

The National Science Digital Library (NSDL) contains digital learning objects and tasks that are related to specific Common Core State Standards for mathematics.

Partnership for Assessment of Readiness for College and Careers Task Prototypes and New Sample Items for Mathematics

www.parcconline.org/samples/math

This page contains sample web-based practice assessment tasks (released items) for your use.

Smarter Balanced Assessment Consortium Sample Items and Performance Tasks

www.smarterbalanced.org/sample-items-and-performance-tasks

This site contains sample higher-level-cognitive-demand tasks and online test-taking and performance-assessment tasks (released items) for your use in class.

Visit **go.solution-tree.com/mathematicsatwork** for continued updates on this resource list.

How the Mathematics at Work High-Leverage Team Actions Support the NCTM Principles to Actions

The *Beyond the Common Core: A Handbook for Mathematics in a PLC at Work* series and the Mathematics at Work process include ten high-leverage team actions teachers should pursue collaboratively every day, in every unit, and every year. The goals of these actions are to eliminate inequities, inconsistencies, and lack of coherence so the focus is on teachers' expectations, instructional practices, assessment practices, and responses to student-demonstrated learning. Therefore, the Mathematics at Work process provides support for NCTM's Guiding Practices for School Mathematics as outlined in the 2014 publication *Principles to Actions: Ensuring Mathematical Success for All* (p. 5). Those principles are:

- **Curriculum principle**—An excellent mathematics program includes a curriculum that develops important mathematics along coherent learning progressions and develops connections among areas of mathematical study and between mathematics and the real world.

- **Professionalism principle**—In an excellent mathematics program, educators hold themselves and their colleagues accountable for the mathematical success of every student and for personal and collective professional growth toward effective teaching and learning of mathematics.

- **Teaching and learning principle**—An excellent mathematics program requires effective teaching that engages students in meaningful learning through individual and collaborative experiences that promote their ability to make sense of mathematical ideas and reason mathematically.

- **Assessment principle**—An excellent mathematics program ensures that assessment is an integral part of instruction, provides evidence of proficiency with important mathematics content and practices, includes a variety of strategies and data sources, and informs feedback to students, instructional decisions, and program improvement.

- **Access and equity principle**—An excellent mathematics program requires that all students have access to a high-quality mathematics curriculum, effective teaching and learning, high expectations, and the support and resources needed to maximize their learning potential.

- **Tools and technology principle**—An excellent mathematics program integrates the use of mathematical tools and technology as essential resources to help students learn and make sense of mathematical ideas, reason mathematically, and communicate their ideas.

Table D.1 (pages 158–159) shows how the HLTAs support NCTM's principles.

Table D.1: The HLTAs and NCTM Principles to Actions

Mathematics At Work High-Leverage Team Actions	NCTM's Guiding Practices for School Mathematics
HLTA 1. Making sense of the agreed-on essential learning standards (content and practices) and pacing What do we want all students in each grade level or course to know, understand, demonstrate, and be able to do? Procedures are in place that ensure teacher teams align the most effective mathematical tasks and instructional strategies to the content progression established in the overall unit plan components.	**Curriculum principle** **Professionalism principle.** The professionalism principle specifically calls for teachers to collaboratively examine and prioritize the mathematics content and Mathematical Practices that students are to learn. **Teaching and learning principle.** The teaching and learning principle establishes mathematics goals to focus learning. **Tools and technology principle**
HLTA 2. Identifying higher-level-cognitive-demand mathematical tasks Teacher teams choose mathematical tasks that represent a balance of higher- and lower-level cognitive demand for the essential learning standards of the unit of study.	**Teaching and learning principle.** Effective teaching and learning practices include implementing tasks that promote reasoning and problem solving and supporting productive struggle in learning mathematics. **Tools and technology principle**
HLTA 3. Developing common assessment instruments Develop, design, and create common end-of-unit assessments as a team before the unit begins based on high-quality design and test-evaluation tools. Ensure the assessment instruments are aligned with the instructional discussions and practices used during the unit and connected to all aspects of the essential learning standards for the unit.	**Assessment principle** **Professionalism principle.** The professionalism principle specifically calls for teachers to collaboratively develop and use common assessments. **Tools and technology principle**
HLTA 4. Developing scoring rubrics and proficiency expectations for the common assessment instruments Design common scoring rubrics and assessment practices to align with expected student reasoning and proficiency for every essential learning standard of the unit.	**Assessment principle**
HLTA 5. Planning and using common homework assignments Homework should be viewed as a daily opportunity for formative self-assessment and independent practice for students. Homework protocols include limiting the number of daily tasks, providing spaced practice, balancing cognitive-demand levels, providing all assignments to the students in advance of the unit, and carefully aligning the essential learning standards for the unit.	**Assessment principle**

HLTA 6. Using higher-level-cognitive-demand mathematical tasks effectively	**Teaching and learning principle.** Effective teaching and learning practices include implementing tasks that promote reasoning and problem solving and supporting productive struggle in learning mathematics.
Teachers provide targeted and differentiated in-class support as students engage in mathematical processes and peer-to-peer discussions for learning by using higher-level-cognitive-demand tasks in every lesson.	**Tools and technology principle**
HLTA 7. Using in-class formative assessment processes effectively	**Assessment principle**
Teacher teams do deep planning for small-group discourse and peer-to-peer in-class formative assessment processes via meaningful, specific, and timely teacher feedback with subsequent student action. This requires much more than the diagnostic tool of checking for understanding. To be formative, students must receive feedback during class and take action on that feedback.	**Teaching and learning principle.** Effective teaching and learning practices include eliciting and using evidence of student thinking.
Teachers intentionally use differentiated and targeted scaffolding and advancing Tier 1 RTI supports as students engage in higher-level-cognitive-demand tasks.	
HLTA 8. Using a lesson-design process for lesson planning and collective team inquiry	**Professionalism principle.** The professionalism principle specifically calls for teachers to collaboratively discuss, select, and implement common research-informed instructional strategies and plans.
Teachers ensure all lesson elements contain successful opportunities for student demonstration of understanding, with feedback and action on student learning.	**Teaching and learning principle.** All lesson designs should draw from the eight research-informed mathematics teaching practices.
Teachers actively engage in a teacher team–developed and team-designed lesson, observe teachers teaching the lesson, and debrief the lesson in order to learn from colleagues.	**Tools and technology principle**
HLTA 9. Ensuring evidence-based student goal setting and action for the next unit of study	**Teaching and learning principle.** Effective teaching and learning practices include eliciting and using evidence of student thinking.
Teachers and teacher teams require students to correct their errors and identify the essential learning standards that are strengths and weaknesses based on the results of the end-of-unit assessment.	**Assessment principle**
Teachers work with students to complete and carry out a plan for improvement and action based on end-of-unit assessment results and outcomes for proficiency.	
HLTA 10. Ensuring evidence-based adult goal setting and action for the next unit of study	**Assessment principle**
Teachers and teacher teams score all end-of-unit assessments together and calibrate scoring to ensure accuracy and freedom from bias.	**Professionalism principle.** The professionalism principle specifically calls for teachers to collaboratively develop action plans that they can implement when students demonstrate that they have or have not attained the standards.
Teachers work together after the unit to determine if proficiency targets for students were achieved.	**Access and equity principle**
Teachers collaboratively and carefully consider how end-of-unit results are used to impact instruction and team planning for the next unit.	

References and Resources

Anderson, J. R., Reder, L. M., & Simon, H. A. (1995). *Applications and misapplications of cognitive psychology to mathematics education.* Unpublished paper, Carnegie Mellon University, Department of Psychology, Pittsburgh, PA. Accessed at http://act.psy.cmu.edu/personal/ja/misapplied.html on July 1, 2014.

Black, P., & Wiliam, D. (2001). *Inside the black box: Raising standards through classroom assessment.* London: Assessment Group of the British Educational Research Association.

Boston, M. D., & Smith, M. S. (2009). Transforming secondary mathematics teaching: Increasing the cognitive demands of instructional tasks used in teachers' classrooms. *Journal for Research in Mathematics Education, 40*(2), 119–156.

Butler, R. (1988). Enhancing and undermining intrinsic motivation: The effects of task-involving and ego-involving evaluation on interest and performance. *British Journal of Educational Psychology, 58*(1), 1–14.

Chappuis, S., & Stiggins, R. J. (2002). Classroom assessment *for* learning. *Educational Leadership, 60*(1), 40–43.

Collins, J., & Hansen, M. T. (2011). *Great by choice: Uncertainty, chaos, and luck—Why some thrive despite them all.* New York: HarperCollins.

Common Core State Standards Initiative. (2014). *Key shifts in mathematics.* Accessed at www.corestandards .org/other-resources/key-shifts-in-mathematics on July 15, 2014.

Conzemius, A. E., & O'Neill, J. (2014). *The handbook for SMART school teams: Revitalizing best practices for collaboration* (2nd ed.). Bloomington, IN: Solution Tree Press.

Cooper, H. (2008a). *Effective homework assignments* (Research brief). Reston, VA: National Council of Teachers of Mathematics.

Cooper, H. (2008b). *Homework: What the research says* (Research brief). Reston, VA: National Council of Teachers of Mathematics.

CTB McGraw-Hill Education LLC. (2014). *Smarter Balanced Assessment Consortium: Practice test scoring guide grade 4 mathematics.* Monterey, CA: Author. Accessed at http://sbac.portal.airast.org /wp-content/uploads/2013/08/G4_Practice-Test-Scoring-Guide-5.14.14-Final.pdf on July 15, 2014.

Darling-Hammond, L. (2014). Testing to, and beyond, the Common Core. *Principal,* 8–12. Accessed at www.naesp.org/sites/default/files/Darling-Hammond_JF14.pdf on February 7, 2014.

Dixon, J. K., & Tobias, J. M. (2013). The "whole" story: Understanding fraction computation. *Mathematics Teaching in the Middle School, 19*(3), 156–163.

DuFour, R., DuFour, R., & Eaker, R. (2008). *Revisiting professional learning communities at work: New insights for improving schools.* Bloomington, IN: Solution Tree Press.

DuFour, R., DuFour, R., Eaker, R., & Karhanek, G. (2010). *Raising the bar and closing the gap: Whatever it takes.* Bloomington, IN: Solution Tree Press.

DuFour, R., DuFour, R., Eaker, R., & Many, T. (2010). *Learning by doing: A handbook for professional learning communities at work* (2nd ed.). Bloomington, IN: Solution Tree Press.

Dweck, C. S. (2007). *Mindset: The new psychology of success.* New York: Ballantine Books.

Fisher, D., Frey, N., & Rothenberg, C. (2010). *Implementing RTI with English learners.* Bloomington, IN: Solution Tree Press.

Frayer, D., Frederick, W. C., & Klausmeier, H. J. (1969). *A schema for testing the level of cognitive mastery.* Madison: Wisconsin Center for Education Research.

Fullan, M. (2008). *The six secrets of change: What the best leaders do to help their organizations survive and thrive.* San Francisco: Jossey-Bass.

Gersten, R., Taylor, M. J., Keys, T. D., Rolfhus, E., & Newman-Gonchar, R. (2014). *Summary of research on the effectiveness of math professional development approaches.* (REL 2014–010). Washington, DC: National Center for Education Evaluation and Regional Assistance.

Gladwell, M. (2008). *Outliers: The story of success.* New York: Little, Brown.

Hattie, J. A. C. (2009). *Visible learning: A synthesis of over 800 meta-analyses relating to achievement.* New York: Routledge.

Hattie, J. A. C. (2012). *Visible learning for teachers: Maximizing impact on learning.* New York: Routledge.

Heflebower, T., Hoegh, J. K., Warrick, P, with Clemens, B., Hoback, M., & McInteer, M. (2014). *A school leader's guide to standards-based grading.* Bloomington, IN: Marzano Research Laboratory.

Herman, J., & Linn, R. (2013). *On the road to assessing deeper learning: The status of Smarter Balanced and PARCC assessment consortia* (CRESST Report 823). Los Angeles: University of California, National Center for Research on Evaluation, Standards, and Student Testing.

Hiebert, J. S., & Grouws, D. A. (2007). The effects of classroom mathematics teaching on students' learning. In F. K. Lester Jr. (Ed.), *Second handbook of research on mathematics teaching and learning: A project of the National Council of Teachers of Mathematics* (pp. 371–404). Charlotte, NC: Information Age.

Hiebert, J., & Stigler, J. W. (2000). A proposal for improving classroom teaching: Lessons from the TIMSS video study. *The Elementary School Journal, 101*(1), 3–20.

Jackson, K., Garrison, A., Wilson, J., Gibbons, L., & Shahan, E. (2013). Exploring relationships between setting up complex tasks and opportunities to learn in concluding whole-class discussions in middle-grades mathematics instruction. *Journal for Research in Mathematics Education, 44*(4), 646–682.

Kanold, T. D. (2011). *The five disciplines of PLC leaders.* Bloomington, IN: Solution Tree Press.

Kanold, T. D. (Ed.), Briars, D. J., Asturias, H., Foster, D., & Gale, M. A. (2013). *Common Core mathematics in a PLC at work, grades 6–8.* Bloomington, IN: Solution Tree Press.

Kanold, T. D., Briars, D. J., & Fennell, F. (2012). *What principals need to know about teaching and learning mathematics.* Bloomington, IN: Solution Tree Press.

Kanold, T. D. (Ed.), Kanold, T. D., & Larson, M. (2012). *Common Core mathematics in a PLC at work, leader's guide.* Bloomington, IN: Solution Tree Press.

Kanold, T. D. (Ed.), Larson, M., Fennell, F., Adams, T. L., Dixon, J. K., Kobett, B. M., & Wray, J. A. (2012a). *Common Core mathematics in a PLC at work, grades K–2.* Bloomington, IN: Solution Tree Press.

Kanold, T. D. (Ed.), Larson, M., Fennell, F., Adams, T. L., Dixon, J. K., Kobett, B. M., & Wray, J. A. (2012b). *Common Core mathematics in a PLC at work, grades 3–5.* Bloomington, IN: Solution Tree Press.

Kanold, T. D. (Ed.), Zimmermann, G., Carter, J., Kanold, T. D., & Toncheff, M. (2012). *Common Core mathematics in a PLC at work, high school.* Bloomington, IN: Solution Tree Press.

Kennedy, M. M. (2010). Attribution error and the quest for teacher quality. *Educational Researcher, 39*(8), 591–598.

Kilpatrick, J., Swafford, J., & Findell, B. (Eds.). (2001). *Adding it up: Helping children learn mathematics.* Washington, DC: National Research Council.

Lappan, G., & Briars, D. (1995). How should mathematics be taught? In Iris M. Carl (Ed.), *Seventy-five years of progress: Prospects for school mathematics* (pp. 131–156). Reston, VA: National Council of Teachers of Mathematics.

Leinwand, S., Brahier, D. J., Huinker, D., Berry III, R. Q., Dillon, F. L., Larson, M. R., et al. (2014). *Principles to actions.* Reston, VA: National Council of Teachers of Mathematics.

Marzano, R. J. (2007). *The art and science of teaching: A comprehensive framework for effective instruction.* Alexandria, VA: Association for Supervision and Curriculum Development.

Marzano, R. J. (2009). *Formative assessment & standards-based grading.* Bloomington, IN: Marzano Research Laboratory.

Morris, A. K., Hiebert, J., & Spitzer, S. M. (2009). Mathematical knowledge for teaching in planning and evaluating instruction: What can preservice teachers learn? *Journal for Research in Mathematics Education, 40*(5), 491–529.

Mueller, C. M., & Dweck, C. S. (1998). Praise for intelligence can undermine children's motivation and performance. *Journal of Personality and Social Psychology, 75*(1), 33–52.

National Board for Professional Teaching Standards. (2010). *National Board for Teacher Certification: Mathematics standards for teachers of students ages 11–18+.* Arlington, VA: Author.

National Council for Teachers of Mathematics. (1991). *Professional standards for teaching mathematics.* Reston, VA: Author.

National Council of Teachers of Mathematics. (2007). *Mathematics teaching today: Improving practice, improving student learning!* Reston, VA: Author.

National Council of Teachers of Mathematics. (2014). *Principles to actions: Ensuring mathematical success for all.* Reston, VA: Author.

National Governors Association Center for Best Practices & Council of Chief State School Officers. (2010). *Common Core State Standards for mathematics.* Washington, DC: Authors. Accessed at www.corestandards.org/assets/CCSSI_Math%20Standards.pdf on February 7, 2014.

O'Neill, J., & Conzemius, A. (2006). *The power of SMART goals: Using goals to improve student learning.* Bloomington, IN: Solution Tree Press.

PARCC. (2013). *Sample mathematics item: Grade 4 "fraction comparison."* Accessed at www.parcconline .org/sites/parcc/files/Grade4-FractionComparison.pdf on September 23, 2014.

Pashler, H., Rohrer, D., & Carpenter, S. K. (2007). Enhancing learning and retarding forgetting: Choices and consequences. *Psychonomic Bulletin & Review, 19*, 187–193.

Popham, W. J. (2011). *Transformative assessment in action: An inside look at applying the process.* Alexandria, VA: Association for Supervision and Curriculum Development.

Reeves, D. (2011). *Elements of grading: A guide to effective practice.* Bloomington, IN: Solution Tree Press.

Resnick, L. B. (Ed.). (2006). Do the math: Cognitive demand makes a difference. *Research Points: Essential Information for Education Policy, 4*(2), 1–4. Accessed at www.aera.net/Portals/38/docs /Publications/Do%20the%20Math.pdf on January 22, 2014.

Rohrer, D., & Pashler, H. (2007). Increasing retention without increasing study time. *Current Directions in Psychological Science, 16*(4). Accessed at www.pashler.com/Articles/RohrerPashler2007CDPS .pdf on March 10, 2014.

Rohrer, D., & Pashler, H. (2010). Recent research on human learning challenges conventional instructional strategies. *Educational Researcher, 39*(5), 406–412.

Silver, E. (2010). Examining what teachers do when they display their best practice: Teaching mathematics for understanding. *Journal of Mathematics Education at Teachers College, 1*(1), 1–6.

Smarter Balanced Assessment Consortium. (2013). *Smarter Balanced Assessment Consortium: Practice test scoring guide—Grade 4.* Accessed at http://sbac.portal.airast.org/wp-content/uploads/2013/07 /Grade4Math.pdf on March 24, 2014.

Smith, M. S., Bill, V., & Hughes, E. (2008). Thinking through a lesson protocol: Successfully implementing higher-level tasks. *Mathematics Teaching in the Middle School, 14*(3), 132–138.

Smith, M. K., Grover, B. W., & Henningsen, M. (1996). Building student capacity for mathematical thinking and reasoning: An analysis of mathematical tasks used in reform classrooms. *American Educational Research Journal, 33*(2), 455–488.

Smith, M. S., & Stein, M. K. (1998). Selecting and creating mathematical tasks: From research to practice. *Mathematics Teaching in the Middle School, 3*(5), 348.

Smith, M. S., & Stein, M. K. (2011). *5 practices for orchestrating productive mathematics discussions.* Thousand Oaks, CA: Corwin Press.

Smith, M. S., & Stein, M. K. (2012). Selecting and creating mathematical tasks: From research to practice. In G. Lappan, M. K. Smith, & E. Jones (Eds.), *Rich and engaging mathematical tasks, grades 5–9* (pp. 344–350). Reston, VA: National Council of Teachers of Mathematics.

Stein, M. K., Remillard, J., & Smith, M. S. (2007). How curriculum influences student learning. In F. Lester (Ed.), *Second handbook of research on mathematics teaching and learning: A project of the National Council of Teachers of Mathematics* (pp. 319–370). Charlotte, NC: Information Age.

Wallace, W. V. (2013). *Formative assessment: Benefit for all.* Unpublished master's thesis, University of Central Florida, Orlando.

Webb, N. L. (1997). *Criteria for alignment of expectations and assessments on mathematics and science education* (Research Monograph No. 6). Washington, DC: Council of Chief State School Officers.

Webb, N. L. (2002). *Depth-of-knowledge levels for four content areas.* Accessed at www.allentownsd.org /cms/lib01/PA01001524/Centricity/Domain/1502/depth%20of%20knowledge%20guide%20for %20all%20subject%20areas.pdf on February 27, 2014.

Wiliam, D. (2007). Keeping learning on track: Classroom assessment and the regulation of learning. In F. K. Lester Jr. (Ed.), *Second handbook of research on mathematics teaching and learning: A project of the National Council of Teachers of Mathematics* (pp. 1051–1098). Charlotte, NC: Information Age.

Wiliam, D. (2011). *Embedded formative assessment.* Bloomington, IN: Solution Tree Press.

Index

Common Core Mathematics in a PLC at Work™ series
Edited by Timothy D. Kanold
By Thomasenia Lott Adams, Harold Asturias, Diane J. Briars, John A. Carter, Juli K. Dixon, Francis (Skip) Fennell, David Foster, Mardi A. Gale, Timothy D. Kanold, Beth McCord Kobett, Matthew R. Larson, Mona Toncheff, Jonathan A. Wray, and Gwendolyn Zimmermann

These teacher guides illustrate how to sustain successful implementation of the Common Core State Standards for mathematics. Discover what students should learn and how they should learn it at each grade level. Comprehensive and research-affirmed analysis tools and strategies will help you and your collaborative team develop and assess student demonstrations of deep conceptual understanding *and* procedural fluency.

BKF566, BKF568, BKF574, BKF561, BKF559

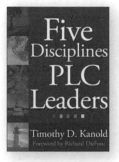

The Five Disciplines of PLC Leaders
By Timothy D. Kanold
Foreword by Richard DuFour

Outstanding leadership in a professional learning community requires practice and patience. Simply trying harder will not yield results; leaders must proactively *train* to get better at the skills that matter. This book offers a framework to focus time, energy, and effort on five key disciplines. Included are reflection exercises to help readers find their own path toward effective PLC leadership.

BKF495

Becoming an Authentic Learning Leader: Whatever You Do, Inspire Me
Featuring Timothy D. Kanold

Encourage your skeptics, cynics, and rebels with Dr. Kanold's eight fundamental disciplines of inspirational leadership. These essential concepts can impact your leadership life as well as the legacy of your leadership team. Practical yet challenging, this humorous and motivational session provides the support and focus needed to sustain effective leadership over time.

DVF063

What Principals Need to Know About Teaching and Learning Mathematics
By Timothy D. Kanold, Diane J. Briars, and Francis (Skip) Fennell

Ensure a challenging mathematics experience for every learner, every day. This must-have resource offers support and encouragement for improved mathematics achievement across every grade level of your school. With an emphasis on *Principles and Standards for School Mathematics* and Common Core State Standards, this book covers the importance of mathematics content, learning and instruction, and mathematics assessment.

BKF501

Solution Tree | Press   *a division of*   Solution Tree   Visit solution-tree.com or call 800.733.6786 to order.